MW01296197

LINUX VIRTUALIZATION

AND

HIGH AVAILABILITY

Prepare for the LPIC-3 304
certification exam

Complete. Quick.

TEACH YOURSELF

LINUX VIRTUALIZATION

AND

HIGH AVAILABILITY

Prepare for the LPIC-3 304
certification exam

Complete. Quick.

David Clinton

Bootstrap IT

www.bootstrap-it.com

info@bootstrap-it.com
www.bootstrap-it.com

ISBN 978-1-365-84720-2

Table of Contents

Introduction

The more cloud-based applications and Internet of Things integration dominate compute models, and the more widespread our access to high-speed network connectivity and cheap data storage, the more critical will it be to have a solid understanding of the inner workings of server virtualization and high availability computing. In a technologically saturated economy, knowledge is king.

If you've decided to read this book, the odds are that you already know that Linux is doing most of the heavy lifting in the world of cloud computing servers. Of the billions of virtual machines and containers launched to provide cloud and clustered services weekly, the vast majority are being run on the Linux kernel.

With all that in mind, the LPIC-3 304 certification provides an excellent framework that can help you build on a solid general background in Linux administration skills, and take the leap and learn how virtualization and high availability actually work.

This book assumes that you are already comfortable working with the basics of Linux management, including file systems, networking, and package management. In fact, in order to earn the LPIC-3 Linux Professional Specialization Certification through any one of its three specialties (300 covers LDAP and Samba, 303 covers security, and 304, virtualization and high availability), you must have already passed the LPIC-1 (Linux Server Professional) and LPIC-2 (Linux Network Professional) levels.

This book also assumes that you're not a complete stranger to the Internet. That's why I didn't see much reason to turn this into some kind of encyclopedia covering every possible configuration scenario and command argument. Besides the fact that no normal reader would be able to make sense of such endless tables of features and commands (much less remember them), having instant access to full details through your favorite search engine means there really isn't any point in including it all here. I also included links to the key documentation pages for each of the technologies I'll be discussing.

But there's a far more important reason that I don't even try to fill my books with "everything": it's because the vast majority of human beings aren't very good at converting buckets full of **information** into useful **skills**. For most people, the most efficient learning process involves actual work in real environments that respond to their actions in real ways (and where there are at least some consequences for failure). Learning is all about struggling to complete practical projects and through investing genuine effort.

What I *have* included in this book is the basic foundation of each technology that you'll need to get off to a quick start. So I'll familiarize you with each technology category and how and why it is normally used, and then introduce you to the two or three leading platforms in that category. I will then describe the key resources you'll need to get a simple deployment up and running. Generally, I'll also provide a quick guide to getting started so you'll be able to visualize the basic steps you'll need. Of course, the LPIC-3 304 exam does cover more than just "getting started", but the material you'll find here should be enough to help you build the working test environments needed to finish the job.

All of which is another way of saying that you should think of "Teach Yourself Linux Virtualization and High Availability" as just one out of the larger set of tools to help you achieve your skill and certification goals.

There's some hard work ahead for you, but I really hope that you'll find that this lightens the load at least a bit. I wish you great success in this journey!

A word about typographical usage: command line examples that do not require admin (sudo) permissions are prefaced with the "$" symbol, while those commands that can only be performed by the admin are prefaced with "#".

I should take this opportunity to express my thanks to G. Matthew Rice, LPI's Executive Director, and especially to Fabian Thorns, LPI's Director of Certification Development, who generously made his immense knowledge and experience available to significantly improve the book's technical quality.

I should also mention the very insightful and helpful review notes I received from Tomas Nevar (of **lisenet.com** - and especially **lisenet.com/lpic-3** - fame).

Finally, this book is licensed under the Creative Commons Attribution license, which means that, in some ways, it will always be a work in progress. If you come across any errors or omissions or feel that you'd like to contribute to improving it, you are most welcome. Please be in touch through the bootstrap-it web site or by email, at info@bootstrap-it.com

The LPIC-3 304 Exam

The Linux Professional Institute has done a particularly good job organizing and defining their exam objectives. Not only can you use the pages on the LPI website as a way to make sure you're not missing anything as you prepare for an exam (the most current version of the LPIC-3 304 exam objectives are here: **wiki.lpi.org/wiki/LPIC-304_Objectives_V2**), but they also happen to work well as a curriculum outline for mastering Linux administration skills in general.

Each objective is given a weight between one and ten. The higher the number, the more significant role a topic will play in the exam (and in your professional life as an administrator). You should take these weights into consideration as you build your "plan of attack" for exam preparation.

Exam Topics:

Objective	Topic	Weight
	Virtualization	
330.1	Virtualization Concepts and Theory	8
330.2	Xen	9
330.3	KVM	9
330.4	Other Virtualization Solutions	3
330.5	Libvirt and Related Tools	5
330.6	Cloud Management Tools	2
	High Availability Cluster Management	
334.1	High Availability Concepts and Theory	5
334.2	Load Balanced Clusters	6
334.3	Failover Clusters	6
334.4	High Availability in Enterprise Linux Distributions	1
	High Availability Cluster Storage	
335.1	DRBD / cLVM	3
335.2	Clustered File Systems	3

1. Virtualization Concepts and Theory

Virtualization

Despite having access to ever more efficient and powerful hardware, operations that are run directly on traditional physical (or bare-metal) servers unavoidably face significant practical limits. The cost and complexity of building and launching a single physical server mean that effectively adding or removing resources to quickly meet changing demand is difficult or, in some cases, impossible. Safely testing new configurations or full applications before their release can also be complicated, expensive, and time-consuming.

As envisioned by pioneering researchers Gerald J. Popek and Robert P. Goldberg in a paper from 1974 ("Formal Requirements for Virtualizable Third Generation Architectures" - Communications of the ACM 17 (7): 412–421), successful virtualization must provide an environment that:

- Is equivalent to that of a physical machine so that software access to hardware resources and drivers should be indistinguishable from a non-virtualized experience.

- Allows complete client control over virtualized system hardware.

- Wherever possible, efficiently executes operations directly on underlying hardware resources, including CPUs.

Virtualization allows physical compute, memory, network, and storage ("core four") resources to be divided between multiple virtual entities. Each virtual device is represented within its software and user environments as an actual, standalone entity. Configured properly, virtually isolated resources can provide more secure applications with no visible connectivity between environments. Virtualization also allows new virtual machines to be provisioned and run almost instantly, and then destroyed as soon as they are no longer needed.

For large applications supporting constantly changing business needs, the ability to quickly scale up and down can spell the difference between survival and failure. The kind of adaptability that virtualization offers allows scripts to add or remove virtual machines in seconds...rather than the weeks it might take to purchase, provision, and deploy a physical server.

How Virtualization Works

Under non-virtual conditions, x86 architectures strictly control which processes can operate within each of four carefully defined privilege layers (described as Ring 0 through Ring 3). Normally, only the host operating system kernel has any chance of accessing instructions kept in Ring 0. However, since you can't give multiple virtual machines running on a single physical computer equal access to ring 0 without asking for big trouble, there must be a virtual machine manager (or "hypervisor") whose job it is to effectively redirect requests for resources like memory and storage to their virtualized equivalents.

When working within a hardware environment without SVM or VT-x virtualization, this is done through a process known as *trap and emulate and binary translation*. On virtualized hardware, such requests can usually be caught by the hypervisor, adapted to the virtual environment, and passed back to the virtual machine.

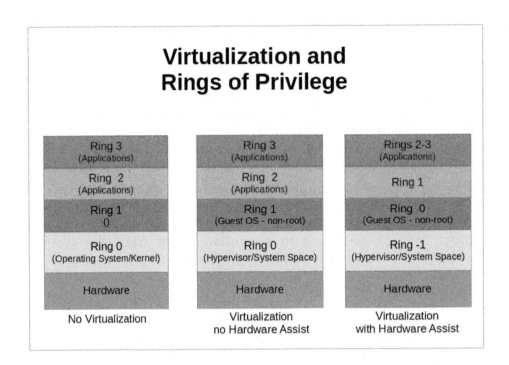

Virtualization and Rings of Privilege

No Virtualization	Virtualization no Hardware Assist	Virtualization with Hardware Assist
Ring 3 (Applications)	Ring 3 (Applications)	Rings 2-3 (Applications)
Ring 2 (Applications)	Ring 2 (Applications)	Ring 1
Ring 1 ()	Ring 1 (Guest OS - non-root)	Ring 0 (Guest OS - non-root)
Ring 0 (Operating System/Kernel)	Ring 0 (Hypervisor/System Space)	Ring -1 (Hypervisor/System Space)
Hardware	Hardware	Hardware

Simply adding a new software layer to provide this level of coordination will add significant latency to just about every aspect of system performance. One very successful solution has been to introduce new instruction sets into CPUs that create a so-called "Ring -1" that will act as Ring 0 and allow a guest OS to operate without having any impact on other, unrelated operations.

In fact, when implemented well, virtualization allows most software code to run exactly the way it normally would without any need for trapping.

Though often playing a support role in virtualization deployments - emulation works quite differently. While virtualization seeks to divide existing hardware resources among multiple users, the goal of emulation is to make one particular hardware/software environment *imitate* one that doesn't actually exist, so that users can launch processes that wouldn't be possible natively. This requires software code that simulates the desired underlying hardware environment to fool your software into thinking it's actually running somewhere else.

Emulation can be relatively simple to implement, but it will nearly always come with a serious performance penalty.

The Hypervisor

Broadly speaking, a hypervisor is a software layer that allocates the hardware resources of a single bare-metal server (a host) among multiple virtualized operating systems (guests). This architecture allows far more efficient use of CPUs, RAM, and storage drives, but does present some added risk of data "leakage" between guests, or unauthorized access to the "physical" Ring 0 of the host kernel).

Therefore, when working with a hypervisor, you should remember that the consequences of a vulnerability affecting the host are far greater than it would be against a stand-alone server, because the host has full access to all of its guests.

You should also create some kind of control mechanism to prevent "server sprawl" - where the ease of spinning up new VMs makes it likely that more and more forgotten and unmanaged guests will end up cluttering the "hallways and closets" of your host machines. Each forgotten VM holds on to its share of resources and exposes more potential security holes.

There have traditionally been two classes of hypervisor: Type-1 and Type-2.

- **Bare-metal hypervisors (Type-1)** are booted as a machine's operating system and – sometimes through a primary privileged virtual machine (VM) – maintain full control over the host hardware, running each guest OS as a system process. XenServer and VMWare ESXi are prominent modern examples of Type-1. In recent years, popular usage of the term "hypervisor" has spread to include all host virtualization technologies, but once upon a time, it would have been used to describe only Type-1 systems. The more general term covering all types would originally have been "Virtual Machine Monitors". Insofar as people use the term Virtual Machine Monitors at all these days, I suspect they mean "hypervisor" in all its iterations.

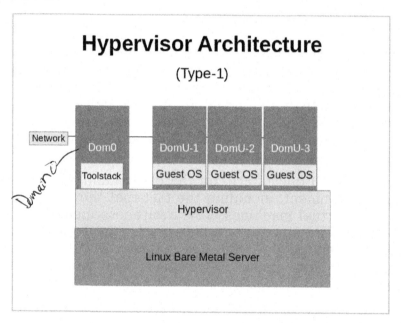

- **Hosted hypervisors (Type-2)** are themselves simply processes running on top of a normal operating system stack. Type-2 hypervisors (which include VirtualBox and, in some ways, KVM) abstract host system resources for guest operating systems, providing the illusion of a private hardware environment.

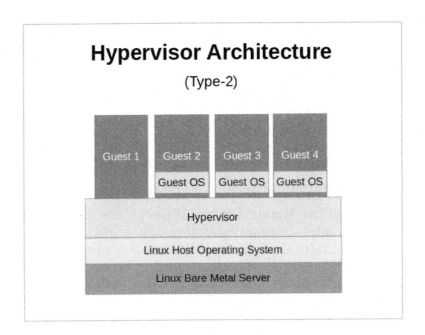

Virtualization: PV vs HVM

Virtual Machines (VMs) are fully virtualized. Or, in other words, they think they're regular operating system deployments living happy lives on their own private hardware. Because they don't need to interface with their environment any differently than a standalone OS, they can run with off-the-shelf unmodified software stacks. In the past, though, this compatibility came at a cost, as translating hardware signals through an emulation layer took extra time and cycles.

Paravirtual (PV) guests are, on the other hand, at least partially aware of their virtual environment, including the fact that they're sharing hardware resources with other virtual machines. This awareness means that there's no need for PV hosts to emulate storage and network hardware and makes efficient I/O drivers available. Historically, this has allowed PV hypervisors to achieve better performance for those operations requiring connectivity to hardware components.

However, to provide guest access to a virtual Ring 0 (i.e., Ring -1), modern hardware platforms - and in particular Intel's Ivy Bridge architecture - introduced a new library of CPU instruction sets that allowed Hardware Virtual Machine (**HVM**) virtualization to leapfrog past the trap-and-emulate bottleneck and take full advantage of hardware extensions and unmodified software kernel operations.

The recent Intel technology, Extended Page Tables (EPT), can also significantly increase virtualization performance.

Therefore, for most use cases, you will now find that HVM provides greater performance, portability, and compatibility.

Hardware Compatibility

At least some virtualization features require hardware support - especially from the host's CPU. Therefore, as we will see in a later chapter, you should make sure that your server has everything you'll need for the task you're going to give it. Most of what you'll need to know is kept in the **/proc/cpuinfo** file and, in particular, in the "flags" section of each processor. Since there will be so many flags however, you'll need to know what to look for.

```
$ grep flags /proc/cpuinfo
flags : fpu vme de pse tsc msr pae mce cx8 apic sep mtrr pge mca
cmov pat pse36 clflush mmx fxsr sse sse2 ht syscall nx mmxext
fxsr_opt pdpe1gb rdtscp lm constant_tsc rep_good nopl nonstop_tsc
extd_apicid aperfmperf pni pclmulqdq monitor ssse3 fma cx16 sse4_1
sse4_2 popcnt aes xsave avx f16c lahf_lm cmp_legacy svm extapic
cr8_legacy abm sse4a misalignsse 3dnowprefetch osvw ibs xop skinit
wdt lwp fma4 tce tbm topoext perfctr_core perfctr_nb arat cpb
hw_pstate npt lbrv svm_lock nrip_save tsc_scale vmcb_clean
flushbyasid decodeassists pausefilter pfthreshold vmmcall bmi1
$
```

The "svm" flag in this output tells me that I've got AMD-V support while "vmx" would indicate the Intel equivalent. In some cases virtualization will be impossible without either svm or vmx, but their absence will always significantly restrict your options.

Container Virtualization

As we've seen, a hypervisor VM is a complete operating system whose relationship to Core Four hardware resources is fully virtualized: it thinks it's running on its own computer.

A hypervisor installs a VM from the same ISO image you would download and use to install an operating system directly onto an empty physical hard drive.

A container, on the other hand is, effectively, an application, launched from a script-like template, that thinks it's an operating system. In container technologies (like LXC and Docker), containers are nothing more than software and resource (files, processes, users) abstractions that rely on the host kernel and a representation of the "core four" hardware resources (i.e, CPU, RAM, network and storage) for everything they do.

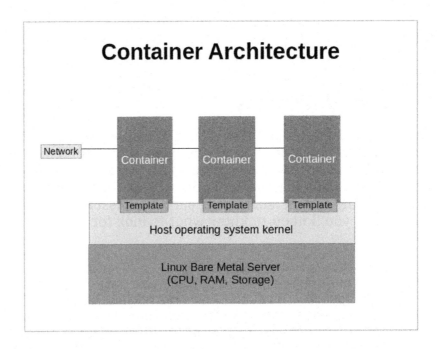

Of course, since containers are, effectively, isolated extensions of the host kernel, virtualizing Windows (or even older or newer Linux releases running incompatible versions of libc) on, say, an Ubuntu 16.04 host, is impossible. But the technology does allow for incredibly lightweight and versatile compute opportunities.

standard C (Libraries)

Migration

The virtualization model also permits a very wide range of migration, backup, and cloning operations – even from running systems (V2V). Since the software resources that define and drive a virtual machine are so easily identified, it usually doesn't take too much effort to duplicate whole server environments in multiple locations and for multiple purposes.

Sometimes it's no more complicated than creating an archive of a virtual file system on one host, unpacking it within the same path on a different host, checking the basic network settings, and firing it up. Most platforms, offer a single command line operation to move guests between hosts. We'll learn more about that later in the book.

Migrating deployments from physical servers to virtualized environments (P2V) can sometimes be a bit more tricky. Even creating a cloned image of a simple physical server and importing it into an empty VM can involve some complexity. And once that's done, you may still need to make considerable adjustments to the design to take full advantage of all the functionality the virtualization has to offer. Depending on the operating system that you are migrating, you might also need to incorporate paravirtualized drivers into the process to allow the OS to run properly in its new home.

As with everything else in server management: carefully plan ahead.

Cloud Service Models

The proliferation of fast and always-on Internet connectivity along with the steadily dropping costs of compute and data services have made it increasingly attractive to outsource data services to cloud providers. Rather than having to estimate potential peak demand levels and then purchase and provision expensive hardware resources to match them, administrators can now consume the services they need when they need them, with no up-front capital expenditure (capex) costs at all.

Advances in server virtualization technologies have made such services practical and, at the same time, provided a business model based on automation and micro-billing that makes it financially attractive. The basic idea is that virtualized units of compute, data, networking, and security tools are purchased as needed and billed per use. Since everything is virtual, scaling up or down is pretty much instant, and can be heavily automated.

Cloud providers like Amazon Web Services, Microsoft's Azure, and the Google Cloud Platform offer services packaged to look and work in ways familiar to server room admins, while providing system-wide integration and geographically distributed duplication that previously couldn't have been imagined. Naturally, it can take some work to configure a particular application to take full advantage of any one cloud provider's peculiar infrastructure.

Cloud services are delivered in many shapes and sizes, and new models appear almost weekly. But there are three industry-changing models that currently dominate the cloud landscape. Let me briefly describe each.

Infrastructure as a Service (IaaS)

IaaS providers like AWS (Elastic Cloud Compute - EC2), Microsoft Azure (Virtual Machines), and the Google Cloud Platform (Compute Engine), offer virtualized compute instances - which themselves mostly run on free Linux hypervisor software like Xen - that come pre-installed and configured with an operating system image of your choice. Instances are often accessible through SSH keys generated by the provider or, in some cases, through keys a user creates and injects into a new instance. When placed within an infrastructure ecosystem including network and firewall services, you are free to do just about anything you want - at any scale you need. You can also build (and share) your own OS images that are optimized specifically for your particular needs.

IaaS providers offer a full range of integrated services alongside their virtual machines, including network, firewall, storage (both block and object), and managed database and deployment tools. The thing to remember about large cloud providers is that, while there is always a physical server running your instance somewhere or other, you'll never know where it is, and you need to concern yourself only with the virtual interface that with which you're presented.

As you might expect, the vast majority of the millions of server instances that are currently running use one flavor or another of Linux.

Platform as a Service (PaaS)

A platform, in the cloud world, is a service that manages your project's underlying infrastructure for you. You can create and manage your own applications on a higher or lower level without having to worry about the compute, network, database, and storage integration details that will make it run. PaaS services will often also help reduce the complexity of many practical details like versioning, collaboration, and testing.

The trade off with PaaS is often in the distance it can place between you and your infrastructure. For instance, you might not be able to connect to your database directly, or some tools with which you're familiar might be unavailable. Before committing to a particular PaaS, you should also make sure that any associated product lock-in won't likely cause you significant trouble down the line.

Getting started with a PaaS might involve selecting a particular software environment like Java, Python, or PHP and uploading your code – which is how Amazon's Elastic Beanstalk works. Or – as with Salesforce.com's Lightening App Builder - it might be a set of abstracted tools from which you can assemble user applications. In many cases, you can pull your application code directly from Git repositories. Either way, you only have to worry about the public function of your application.

Other significant PaaS providers include Google App Engine, Heroku, and Cloud Foundry.

Software as a Service (SaaS)

Many of the most widely-used cloud-based tools fall into the category of SaaS, because they are provided as complete services. Good examples of such centrally hosted and licensed services include Google's Gmail and Drive and the WordPress web publishing platform, all of which are persistently available for immediate, on-demand use by consumers, either individually, or through enterprise accounts.

Virtualization Best Practices

Despite all that virtualization can deliver, caution is still your most valuable administration tool. Security threats won't somehow miraculously dissolve when they encounter a virtual machine, weak passwords don't become safer just because they're being used on containers, and operating systems won't patch themselves (unless you tell them to).

There are, however, plenty of design considerations that are unique to virtual operations. It's a good idea, for instance, to carefully assess whether your applications will work well in a virtual world...and then which particular technology platform is the best fit (working through the practical "getting started" guides in this book is a great way to get to know your options better).

You will probably want to start off small: test your design on just a subset of your total infrastructure and gradually expand its adoption. Compartmentalizing your resources by keeping data stores and databases separate from your VMs can add resilience and efficiencies to your deployments and reduce the damage from failure.

And, above all, plan and test everything before deploying to make sure that you will actually provide the performance and connectivity you need.

Test Yourself

1. Which of the following most accurately describes a Type-1 hypervisor?

a) A software layer running distinct VM processes.

b) A software stack with direct control over the host hardware.

c) A kernel hypervisor with no need for a host OS at all.

d) A virtual machine (VM).

2. Which of the following is an example of a Type2 hypervisor?

a) LynxSecure

b) Xen

c) KVM

d) VMWare ESXi

3. Which VMs are more likely to be aware of the physical hardware resources on their hosts?

a) Paravirtual (PV)

b) Hardware Virtual Machines (HVM)

c) LXC

d) Docker

4. How would you most accurately characterize a cloud service offering full access to the operating systems of virtual machines?

a) IaaS

b) PaaS

c) Saas

d) Hypervisors

5. Which of the following CPU flags is particularly important for virtualization considerations?

a) lm

b) aes

c) svm

d) apicid

Answer Key: 1:b,2:c,3:a,4:a,5:c

2. Xen

LPIC-304 Exam Objective 330.2

Architecture
Installation
Create a PV (Paravirtualized) Guest
Create an HVM (Hardware Virtualized) Guest
Xen File Locations
Administration
Migration

As we've seen, the virtualization of compute resources can deliver enormous practical and economic benefits. And as we've also seen, I'm not the first person to figure that out: most of the Internet - fueled by that part of it that we call "the cloud" - is heavily virtualized. In this chapter, we'll learn how to use what is surely one of the most widely adopted virtual resource managers of them all: Xen.

When you install Xen, it loads its management tools and a Xen kernel. This kernel will be added to the available boot candidates in your GRUB configuration and, whenever it's selected at boot time, Xen will launch a virtual machine called Dom0 (or sometimes, "Domain 0") that will manage all future VMs. Dom0 is the only domain given system privileges.

From a practical perspective, what this means is that Xen isn't just a process running on top of Linux but, in fact, lives right on the bare metal hardware server. It's important to remember that Xen enjoys direct access to all your hardware resources. Xen fully supports both Paravirtual (PV) and Hardware Virtual Machine (HVM) models.

Until relatively recently, successfully installing Xen required modifications to the Linux kernel. Since Linux kernel 3.0, however, many Linux distributions now ship with a specially patched kernel that will fully support Xen. Exceptions to this include CentOS (which shares the Red Hat Enterprise software stack) that, since Red Hat dropped Xen support with version 6, requires manual modifications via packages from the CentOS-Extras repository before Xen will load. Full documentation is available from a number of sources, including https://wiki.centos.org/HowTos/Xen/Xen4QuickStart.

We'll get to the installation process in just a moment, but first let's take a quick look at the way a Xen hypervisor is built.

The guest operating systems (VMs) created and managed by Xen are known as domU - or, Unprivileged - domains. Depending on whether they're created with HVM or PV architectures, domU guests will be either more or less aware of their underlying hardware, but they'll all be restricted to a very carefully defined range of resources.

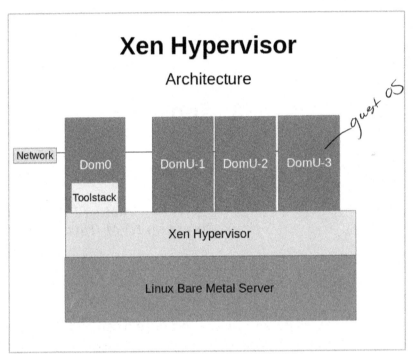

Installation

Preparing Your Partitions

Assuming that you've already enabled virtualization support at the BIOS level on the computer you're using for a server (which, depending on your system and the virtualization method you're planning to use, might appear in the BIOS menu as something like "Enable Virtualization Technology" or "Enable Intel VT"), you'll need to install Linux.

The installation will work as normal except for the disk partitions: you'll still create the regular partitions for root (/), swap, and /boot, but you'll also need an unused partition - using either the LVM (Logical Volume Manager) or a file system to store disk images associated with guests as files using raw, qcow2, or vhd formats. This is the space we'll later use for our guest virtual machines (VMs). You will also need at least one operating system image file - usually a .iso file downloaded from the distribution web site - to run on your VM.

Once Linux is running, you will install LVM - the Logical Volume Manager - to work with this partition.

Distribution	Package Name
Debian	lvm2
CentOS	lvm*
SuSE	(Included)

To prepare the disk for Xen, you can use **pvcreate** to configure our LVM-ready volume to store the partition's blocks (known as extents). This example assumes that the LVM partition was designated as sda5.

Partition create for LVM

```
# pvcreate /dev/sda5
```

Then you'll create a volume group called, say, 'vg0XenGuest' out of the LVM volume.

create volume group

```
# vgcreate vg0XenGuest /dev/sda5
```

From here on in, you can use LVs for all your Xen storage volumes. LVM-based partitions can be divided into multiple block devices and shared among guests according to your specific needs. You should be careful to anticipate your future LVM volume demands and incorporate them into your pre-installation partition design.

Setting up a Network Bridge

The most common way of dealing with the peculiarities and complexities of Xen networking involves creating a bridge device as a kind of network switch through which your guests will connect to the outside world. The bridge which, by default, is called xenbr0 will live within the Dom0 VM and will be bound directly to a physical, Internet-connected interface. All network traffic into and out of your guest VMs will route through the xenbr0 bridge.

If Network Manager happens to be running on your system, you'll need to make sure that it's not trying to control any of the interfaces you're going to be working with. It will usually make sense to disable Network Manager altogether:

Ubuntu 15.04+ CentOS 7+ Debian 8+:	systemctl stop NetworkManager
Ubuntu 14.04:	stop network-manager
Debian 7:	/etc/init.d/network-manager stop

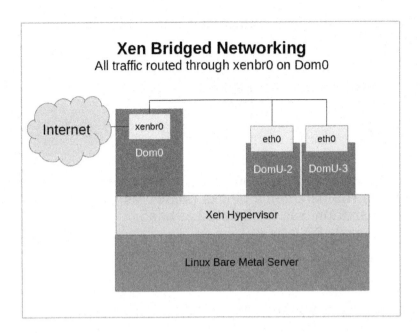

Debian/Ubuntu

To do this on Debian and Ubuntu - we'll get to RHEL/CentOS in just a minute - you'll need to install the **bridge-utils** package and then manually add a bridge device to the interfaces file and launch it. You will need to edit the /etc/network/interfaces file to look like this:

```
auto lo
iface lo inet loopback

auto eth0
iface eth0 inet manual

auto xenbr0
iface xenbr0 inet dhcp
    bridge_ports eth0
```

With the **bridge_ports eth0** line, you are telling the system to enslave a virtual interface (here named eth0) to the bridge. In this case, we will use DHCP to get an IP address for our bridge, which will forward traffic to the guest's eth0 interface.

Make sure you've got a Plan B for connecting with your machine in case something goes wrong, and restart your network:

```
# ifdown eth0 && ifup xenbr0
```

If everything worked according to plan, you should now have full network access.

RHEL/CentOS

If you're on Red Hat or CentOS, you'll need to create two ifcfg configuration files in the **/etc/sysconfig/network-scripts/** directory: one (which we'll call ifcfg-eth0) as a physical network device on the bridge, and the second (ifcfg-xenbr0) to define the bridge itself and its IP network. Naturally, you'll edit the HWADDR value to match your NIC's actual address.

/etc/sysconfig/network-scripts/ifcfg-eth0

```
DEVICE=eth0
HWADDR=00:16:76:D6:C9:45
ONBOOT=yes
BRIDGE=xenbr0
NM_CONTROLLED=no
```

/etc/sysconfig/network-scripts/ifcfg-xenbr0

```
DEVICE=xenbr0
TYPE=Bridge
BOOTPROTO=dhcp
ONBOOT=yes
DELAY=0
NM_CONTROLLED=no
```

We're now ready to actually install Xen itself (along with xen-utils).

Distribution	Package Name
Ubuntu:	xen-system-amd64
Debian:	xen-linux-system.
CentOS:	yum groupinstall 'Virtualization'
	yum install xen

You'll need to reboot before the Xen image is loaded. You can, by the way, closely control the parameters used by Xen as it loads by editing its GRUB menu item – or, on most distributions, through the **/etc/default/grub** file (although it does sometimes appear as **/boot/grub/grub.conf**). The GRUB configuration file is also where you set the default boot target.

```
            GNU GRUB  version 2.02~beta2-9ubuntu1.7

 ┌─────────────────────────────────────────────────────────────────────┐
 │ Ubuntu                                                                │
 │ Advanced options for Ubuntu                                           │
 │*Ubuntu GNU/Linux, with Xen hypervisor                                 │
 │ Advanced options for Ubuntu GNU/Linux (with Xen hypervisor)           │
 │ Memory test (memtest86+)                                              │
 │ Memory test (memtest86+, serial console 115200)                       │
 │                                                                       │
 │                                                                       │
 │                                                                       │
 │                                                                       │
 │                                                                       │
 │                                                                       │
 └─────────────────────────────────────────────────────────────────────┘

      Use the ↑ and ↓ keys to select which entry is highlighted.
      Press enter to boot the selected OS, `e' to edit the commands
      before booting or `c' for a command-line.
```

You can control how Xen boots by adding parameters to the GRUB configuration, including adding, as an example, **dom0_mem=800M** to the kernel line to restrict dom0 to 800 MB memory , and **dom0_max_vcpus=2** to limit the number of CPUs visible to dom0.

Note from the screenshot of the GRUB edit page that follows how, in the "multiboot" line, Xen loads first, and is followed by the operating system (in the "module" lines):

```
                  GNU GRUB  version 2.02~beta2-9ubuntu1.7

 ┌─────────────────────────────────────────────────────────────────────────┐
 │e-891d49c1802b                                                           ↑│
 │        fi                                                                │
 │        echo          'Loading Xen 4.4-amd64 ...'                         │
 │        if [ "$grub_platform" = "pc" -o "$grub_platform" = "" ]; then     │
 │            xen_rm_opts=                                                   │
 │        else                                                              │
 │            xen_rm_opts="no-real-mode edd=off"                            │
 │        fi                                                                │
 │        multiboot          /xen-4.4-amd64.gz placeholder   ${xen_rm_opts} │
 │        echo          'Loading Linux 4.2.0-27-generic ...'                │
 │        module          /vmlinuz-4.2.0-27-generic placeholder root=UUID=3e\│
 │1acf69-b84d-4e7e-ba75-eff416c32ff3 ro                                     │
 │        echo          'Loading initial ramdisk ...'                       │
 │        module          --nounzip  /initrd.img-4.2.0-27-generic           │
 │ _                                                                        │
 └─────────────────────────────────────────────────────────────────────────┘

    Minimum Emacs-like screen editing is supported. TAB lists
    completions. Press Ctrl-x or F10 to boot, Ctrl-c or F2 for a
    command-line or ESC to discard edits and return to the GRUB
    menu.
```

Create a PV (Paravirtualized) Guest

Creating a new PV guest operating system is a two step process. You first need
to generate a .cfg file, and then use the **xl create** command to read the file and
load the guest. You could write the .cfg file by hand, but we'll install xen-tools to
do it for us through **xen-create-image**, which takes a number of parameters as
input:

```
# xen-create-image --lvm=vg0XenGuest \
  --hostname=myNewGuest \
  --memory=512mb \
  --vcpus=2 \
  --lvm=vg0 \
  --dhcp \
  --pygrub \
  --dist=xenial
```

In this case, we'll use myNewGuest as a **hostname** and 512MB for **memory**. We'll assign our guest two virtual CPUs (**vcpus**), receive an IP address through an available DHCP server, control the boot process with pygrub, and - most important of all - use Ubuntu 16.04 (known as Xenial) as a guest operating system (**dist**).

You should be curious about where the source image that will make up this operating system is going to come from. And you should be just as curious to know if there are any other OSs available that we could choose. The answer to both is: **/usr/share/xen-tools/**

```
/usr/share/xen-tools$ ls
centos-4.d   fedora-core-11.d fedora-core-7.d  karmic.d    saucy.d
centos-5.d   fedora-core-12.d fedora-core-8.d  lenny.d     sid.d
centos-6.d   fedora-core-13.d fedora-core-9.d  lucid.d     squeeze.d
common       fedora-core-14.d feisty.d         maverick.d  stable.d
common.sh    fedora-core-15.d gentoo.d         natty.d     testing.d
dapper.d     fedora-core-16.d gutsy.d          oneiric.d   trusty.d
debian.d     fedora-core-17.d hardy.d          precise.d   wheezy.d
edgy.d       fedora-core-4.d  intrepid.d       quantal.d   etch.d
fedora-core-5.d               jaunty.d         raring.d    fedora-core-
10.d
fedora-core-6.d               jessie.d         sarge.d
/usr/share/xen-tools$
```

These directories contain the scripts Xen needs to properly provision guest domains running any of these distribution versions. Naturally, you can manually build your own, but that's a bit beyond the scope of this book - although you can find a pretty good guide for that here:

wiki.alpinelinux.org/wiki/Create_Alpine_Linux_PV_DomU

After **xen-create-image** finishes building your instance, an installation summary will be displayed in your terminal that includes the root password. You will soon use that to log in. At that point, you might want to create a new admin user and log in again with that account, exercising admin rights only through sudo.

For each new guest configuration that it creates, the **xen-create-image** program produces a .cfg (configuration) file in the **/etc/xen/** directory. The file is named after the hostname you specified and, in our case, will look something like this:

```
# Configuration file for the Xen instance myNewGuest, created
# by xen-tools 4.4 on Mon Feb 29 14:06:24 2016.
# kernel + memory size
bootloader = '/usr/lib/xen-4.4/bin/pygrub'

vcpus       = '2'
memory      = '512'

#  Disk device(s).
root        = '/dev/xvda2 ro'
disk        = [
                'phy:/dev/vg0/myNewGuest-disk,xvda2,w',
                'phy:/dev/vg0/myNewGuest-swap,xvda1,w',
              ]
# Physical volumes
#
# Hostname
#
name        = 'myNewGuest'
# Networking
#
dhcp        = 'dhcp'
vif         = [ 'mac=00:16:3E:59:A0:CD' ]
# Behaviour
#
on_poweroff = 'destroy'
on_reboot   = 'restart'
on_crash    = 'restart'
```

Notice how the file points to the absolute location of the bootloader (pygrub) and sets the "disk" property to match the two LV partitions (xvda1 and xvda2) that we assigned. Xen will have the guest's Linux root directory (built from the Ubuntu Trusty image defined in **xen-create-image**) installed to **/dev/xvda2**.

You're probably wondering where some of the .cfg parameters we didn't specify from the command line (like volume size, for instance) came from. The answer? All default values are taken from the **/etc/xen-tools/xen-tools** file. Here are some settings and comments from that file:

```
#  Output directory for storing loopback images.
# dir = /home/xen

# If you don't wish to use loopback images then you may specify an
# LVM volume group here instead
# lvm = vg0

#  Installation method.
# install-method = [ debootstrap | rinse | rpmstrap | copy | tar ]
install-method = debootstrap


#
# If you're using the "copy", or "tar" installation methods you
# need to specify the source location to copy from, or the source
# .tar file to unpack.
#
# You may specify that with a line such as:
#
# install-source = /path/to/copy
# install-source = /some/path/img.tar
##
#  Disk and Sizing options.
size    = 4G        # Root disk, suffix (G, M, k) required
memory = 128M      # Suffix (G, M, k) required
#maxmem = 256M      # Suffix (G, M, k) optional
swap    = 128M      # Suffix (G, M, k) required
# noswap = 1        # Don't use swap at all for new systems.
fs      = ext3      # Default file system for any disk
dist    = `xt-guess-suite-and-mirror --suite`

# Networking setup values.
#
# gateway    = 192.168.1.1
# netmask    = 255.255.255.0
# broadcast  = 192.168.1.255
# Uncomment this if you wish the images to use DHCP:
# dhcp = 1

# nameserver = 192.168.1.1
# bridge = xendmz

#  Uncomment if you wish newly created images to boot once they've
# been created.
# boot = 1
```

Let's explain some of those settings a bit. While the default is debootstrap (a clever tool for installing an OS directly from a network repository), you can choose an **install-method** for guests based on source files using either **tar** or **copy**, in which case you'll need to specify your source (**install-source**); or by using the **rinse** or **rpmstrap** commands (both of which are inspired by debootstrap).

Size (for disk size), **memory**, and **swap** obviously all allow you to define the way Xen will provision those details. You've got a full range of networking settings and the option of automatically booting a new image.

With the .cfg file all ready, there's nothing for us to do besides pull the trigger and launch our guest.

```
# xl create -c /etc/xen/myNewGuest.cfg
```

-c will open a shell in the new guest so you can perform any administration tasks that haven't yet been applied. Running xl console against either the domain ID Xen gave it during creation or the hostname you specified will similarly open a new session:

```
# xl console 1
```

For some reason, you can't close a console session using the traditional **exit**. Instead, that will require CTRL+].

Here's a look at how networking can appear from within a guest domain's **/etc/network/interfaces** file:

```
ubuntu@ubuntu-template: /etc/xen

File Edit View Search Terminal Help
root@myNewerGuest:/etc/network# cat interfaces
# This file describes the network interfaces available on your system
# and how to activate them. For more information, see interfaces(5).

# The loopback network interface
auto lo
iface lo inet loopback

# The primary network interface
auto eth0
iface eth0 inet dhcp
# post-up ethtool -K eth0 tx off

#
# The commented out line above will disable TCP checksumming which
# might resolve problems for some users.  It is disabled by default
#
root@myNewerGuest:/etc/network#
```

Create an HVM (Hardware Virtualized) Guest

Creating HVM guests requires a bit more manual intervention than PV. We'll need to create our own virtual device on the vg0 volume group called, say, ubuntu_hmv.

```
# lvcreate -n ubuntu_hmv -L 5G vg0
```

Now you will download an ISO image of the operating system you want to use and place it in an accessible directory. Keeping in mind the path to the ISO, create a file called ubuntu-hmv.cfg in the **/etc/xen/** directory and add these contents (appropriately adapted for your environment):

```
builder = "hvm"
name = "ubuntu-hvm"
memory = "512"
vcpus = 1
vif = ['bridge=xenbr0']
disk = ['phy:/dev/vg0/ubuntu-hvm,hda,w','file:/home/ubuntu/ubuntu-
16.04-desktop-amd64.iso,hdc:cdrom,r']
vnc = 1
boot="dc"
```

When that's done, you can create your guest:

```
# xl create /etc/xen/ubuntu-hvm.cfg
```

Use a local vnc viewer on your own workstation to attach to the instance and work through the installation process.

```
$ vncviewer localhost:0
```

For virtual desktop access to HVM guests, you can also use a properly installed SPICE protocol viewer and, rather than **vnc = 1**, point to it from your .cfg file using:

```
spice=BOOLEAN
```

Whichever software you use to connect to your guest, if you'll be working by way of an insecure network (like the Internet), you'll need to encrypt the connection.

An SSH tunnel is perfect for this purpose. Creating and then using that tunnel might look like this:

```
$ ssh -l <username> -L 5910:localhost:5910 <hostname>
vncviewer localhost::5910
```

Just as you would remove the CDRom from the drive once your installation to a physical system is complete, you will need to remove the virtual CDRom before you can boot this guest again. Therefore, edit the "**disk=**" line to look like this:

```
disk = ['phy:/dev/vg0/ubuntu-hvm,hda,w']
```

To remove a CDRom drive from within your guest, you can simply use **eject**. **eject -t** will tell your guest to look for a new CD.

```
eject
eject -t
```

Pre-Built Images

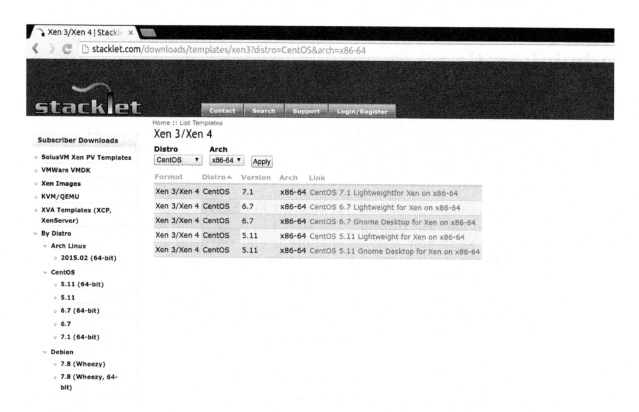

If you'd rather not roll your own, there are all kinds of public Xen images that you can simply download. Stacklet.com, for instance, allows you to browse through and select from available images by distribution, format, and architecture.

Once you've downloaded an image archive to a working Xen environment, you uncompress the package (which will probably contain one .img and one .cfg file), edit the .cfg file to point to your image, and run something like:

```
# xl create -c centos-6.7-x86-64.pygrub.cfg
```

Xen File Locations

We've already seen how xen-tools keeps scripts for creating and running common Linux distributions in **/usr/share/xen-tools/**. But there are some other Xen-related configuration directories and files you should know about.

/etc/xen/ is home to the .cfg files you'll use to create your guests, along with sample guest configuration files (for both pv and hvm domains), the **xl.conf** file, and .sxp files - which are configuration files for either the **xm** or **xend** toolstack.

The files containing user data for your guest configurations can be found in **/var/lib/xen/**, **/var/lib/xen-4.4/** contains Xen binaries and shared libraries, and Xen logs are written to **/var/log/xen/**. You can place symbolic links to guest .cfg files into the **/etc/xen/auto/** directory to have them load on system boot.

Administration

Toolstacks

The active toolstack currently available within a Xen environment is determined by the value of the TOOLSTACK= line in the **/etc/default/xen** file. xm, xl, and XAPI are possible values although, as we've already seen, xm has been largely replaced by xl.

XAPI (the management tool for Citrix's XenServer), on the other hand, deserves some attention as, through its xe CLI, it is the main API interface to Xen resources. xe, when XAPI is installed, can be used from both dom0 and from remote hosts, over https. xe's scripting capabilities make it particularly useful for integrating virtual and physical resources.

Note: previous to XenServer version 6.2, you would be required to activate a free license each year to run the standard edition. Since then, Citrix has made the entire core XenServer project open source.

xl

xl will probably be the tool you'll use most often. xl recently replaced the older xm tool as the default Xen management shell. In case you're worried, xl commands are largely backwards compatible with xm.

Once you're in a Xen host shell, you can use any xl command to confirm that Xen is behaving the way it should. **xl list**, for instance, will list all the existing guests (or, domains) on your system. The domain ID is the number a particular guest has been assigned and can be used with other commands to identify a domain.

```
ubuntu@ubuntu:~# xl list
Name                               ID    Mem VCPUs    State    Time(s)
Domain-0                            0   1351     1    r-----      19.9
myNewGuest                          1    512     2    -b----       0.2
ubuntu@ubuntu:~$
```

xl info will display information about your Xen environment:

```
ubuntu@ubuntu:~# xl info
host                   : ubuntu
release                : 4.2.0-27-generic
version                : #32~14.04.1-Ubuntu SMP Fri Jan 22 15:32:26
UTC 2016
machine                : x86_64
nr_cpus                : 1
max_cpu_id             : 0
nr_nodes               : 1
cores_per_socket       : 1
threads_per_core       : 1
cpu_mhz                : 3905
hw_caps                :
078bf3ff:2b93fb7f:00000000:00000400:00000201:00000000:00000011:0000
0000
virt_caps              :
total_memory           : 2047
free_memory            : 159
sharing_freed_memory   : 0
sharing_used_memory    : 0
outstanding_claims     : 0
free_cpus              : 0
xen_major              : 4
xen_minor              : 4
xen_extra              : .2
xen_version            : 4.4.2
xen_caps               : xen-3.0-x86_64 xen-3.0-x86_32p
xen_scheduler          : credit
xen_pagesize           : 4096
platform_params        : virt_start=0xffff800000000000
xen_changeset          :
xen_commandline        : placeholder
cc_compiler            : gcc (Ubuntu 4.8.2-19ubuntu1) 4.8.2
cc_compile_by          : stefan.bader
cc_compile_domain      : canonical.com
cc_compile_date        : Wed Feb 24 21:00:00 UTC 2016
xend_config_format     : 4
ubuntu@ubuntu:~$
```

You can open a console session in a guest domain using xl console:

```
# xl console myNewGuest
```

xl shutdown will, when run from Domain0, shut myNewGuest down. You can completely delete a domain using **xl destroy**.

```
# xl shutdown myNewGuest
# xl destroy MyNewGuest
```

Here are some common **xe** command line operations. You can start a VM using **vm-start**:

```
# xe vm-start vm=<VM name>
```

This will list all the available networks:

```
# xe network-list
```

You can create a new network with **network-create**:

```
# xe network-create name-label=<mynetworkname>
```

Use **vm-cd-add** to designate an existing drive as a virtual CDRom for a VM:

```
# xe vm-cd-add cd-name=MyVirtualCD vm=MyVMName device=/dev/sda
```

When something's gone wrong and there's no other way out (short of physically rebooting your server), try a restart:

```
# xe-toolstack-restart
```

Once you're done with a VM, destroy it this way:

```
# xe vm-destroy uuid=<UUID>
```

Running...

```
# xe vm-list
```

...from domain0 will list all local VMs. To accomplish the same thing from a remote computer (with the xe-cli installed), use something like this:

```
# xe -s 55.211.34.9 -u ubuntu -pw mypassword vm-list
```

To resize a disk that's already in use by a virtual machine, shut down the VM and get the disk's Virtual Disk Image's UUID by running this:

```
# xe vm-disk-list vm=<vm name>
```

You can then resize the VDI, specifying the unit of size using either GiB or MiB:

```
# xe vdi-resize uuid=<vdi uuid> size=<size>
```

Monitoring

If you've got dozens or even hundreds of VMs running, you'll need tools for keeping up with everything that's happening. **xentop** displays usage data on your guests much the same way that **top** does on normal systems.

```
# xentop
```

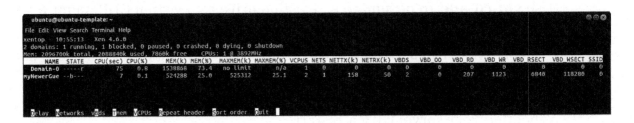

You can troubleshoot problems with both the creation and running of guests using **xl dmesg** - especially when you run it immediately after booting the Xen kernel:

```
ubuntu@ubuntu:~# xl dmesg
(XEN)    Xen    version    4.4.2    (Ubuntu    4.4.2-0ubuntu0.14.04.5)
(stefan.bader@canonical.com) (gcc (Ubuntu 4.8.2-19ubuntu1) 4.8.2)
debug=n Wed Feb 24 21:00:00 UTC 2016
(XEN) Bootloader: GRUB 2.02~beta2-9ubuntu1.7
(XEN) Command line: placeholder
(XEN) Video information:
(XEN)    VGA is text mode 80x25, font 8x16
(XEN) Disc information:
(XEN)    Found 1 MBR signatures
(XEN)    Found 1 EDD information structures
(XEN) Xen-e820 RAM map:
(XEN)    0000000000000000 - 000000000009fc00 (usable)
(XEN)    000000000009fc00 - 00000000000a0000 (reserved)
(XEN)    00000000000f0000 - 0000000000100000 (reserved)
(XEN)    0000000000100000 - 000000007fff0000 (usable)
(XEN)    000000007fff0000 - 0000000080000000 (ACPI data)
(XEN)    00000000fffc0000 - 0000000100000000 (reserved)
(XEN) System RAM: 2047MB (2096700kB)
(XEN) ACPI: RSDP 000E0000, 0024 (r2 VBOX   )
(XEN) ACPI: XSDT 7FFF0030, 003C (r1 VBOX   VBOXXSDT 1 ASL        61)
(XEN) ACPI: FACP 7FFF00F0, 00F4 (r4 VBOX VBOXFACP   1 ASL        61)
(XEN) ACPI: DSDT 7FFF0470, 1BF1 (r1 VBOX   VBOXBIOS 2 INTL 20140214)
(XEN) ACPI: FACS 7FFF0200, 0040
(XEN) ACPI: APIC 7FFF0240, 0054 (r2 VBOX VBOXAPIC 1 ASL        61)
(XEN) ACPI: SSDT 7FFF02A0, 01CC (r1 VBOX VBOXCPUT 2 INTL 20140214)
[…]
ubuntu@ubuntu:~#
```

To illustrate how this can work in the real world, while having trouble creating an HVM guest on a VirtualBox-based deployment of Xen, I was given this **xl dmesg** output:

```
hvm.c:544:d0 Attempt to create a HVM guest on a non-VT/AMDV
platform.
```

...which told me that, for some reason or other, VirtualBox wasn't providing suitable virtualization support at the BIOS level. Without such support, it will be impossible to load HVM guests.

The **xenstored** daemon maintains configuration and status data on all domain devices attached to Xen domains. The key/value pairs that xenstore holds represent those devices, which rely on xenstore to keep them isolated from each other. **xenstore-ls** will list keys, values and permissions. An excerpt of its output might look like this:

```
# xenstore-ls
[...]
vm = ""
 00000000-0000-0000-0000-000000000000 = ""
  memory = "1502"
 c1c0c3c1-ba4c-4828-a4cd-bf5e320d1cfc = ""
  name = "myNewGuest"
  uuid = "c1c0c3c1-ba4c-4828-a4cd-bf5e320d1cfc"
  image = ""
   ostype = "linux"
  start_time = "1464530239.61"
libxl = ""
 1 = ""
  dm-version = "qemu_xen"
#
```

xenstore-exists <keyname> will test for the existence of a key, xenstore-read <keyname> will read its value, and xenstore-rm <keyname> will remove it.

Hotplugging

You can add or remove individual devices or even virtual CPUs while a domain is running using what's called hotplugging. In these examples, "1" is the domain ID and guest-volume is the new block device.

block-list, followed by a domain ID, will list all the block devices currently attached to the domain:

```
# xl block-list 1
Vdev  BE  handle state evt-ch ring-ref BE-path
51714 0 1 4 17 8 /local/domain/0/backend/vbd/1/
51714 51713 0 1 4 18 9 /local/domain/0/backend/vbd/1/51713
#
```

You can then use either block-attach or block-detach to add or remove devices.

```
# xl block-attach 1 /dev/vg/guest-volume,,hda
# xl block-detach <domain-id> <device-id>
```

Similarly, you can list networks by domain using network-list:

```
# xl network-list 1
Idx  BE  Mac  Addr.  handle  state  evt-ch  tx-/rx-ring-ref  BE-path
0    0      00:16:3e:6f:2b:c1      0      4      -1      11/10
/local/domain/0/backend/vif/1/0
#
```

network-attach and **network-detach** can be used to manage networks:

```
# xl network-attach 1 <device>
# xl network-detach 1 /local/domain/0/backend/vif/1/0
```

CPU Management

On NUMA (Non-Uniform Memory Access) systems, there can be large differences between CPU-memory access times depending on the relative distance between a given CPU and the memory it's trying to access. To deal with possible performance deficiencies, Xen allows you to manage connections between guest domains and specific CPUs. First of all, you can display your NUMA status through xl info:

```
ubuntu@ubuntu-template:~# xl info -n
[...]
numa_info            :
node:    memsize    memfree    distances
   0:      6144       5754      10,20
   1:      6720       5850      20,10
ubuntu@ubuntu-template:~#
```

You can associate a new domain with specific CPUs (called "node affinity") by pinning vCPUs to specified pCPUs as domains are created. Including these lines in your domain creation, for instance, would "pin" all for vCPUs given the domain to pCPUs numbers 0-3. This will associate your domain to any or all NUMA nodes to which those pCPUs belong.

```
vcpus =  '4'
memory =  '1024'
cpus = "0-3"
```

From Xen version 4.3 and up, you can specify *preferred* pCPUs even within a given NUMA node...while they will still run on any available pCPU should the preferred one be unavailable. This is called NUMA Aware Scheduling. This example will "pin" Guest1 to physical CPU 1:

```
xl vcpu-pin Guest1 1 1
```

You can also increase or decrease the number of vCPUs available to an existing domain using **xl vcpu-set**. This example will assign two vCPUs to domain 1:

```
# xl vcpu-set 1 2
```

Migration

Should the need arise (and, over time, it almost certainly will), you can easily migrate a running domain from one physical hypervisor server to another. A common use-case might involve a domain running on a host that needs to be shut down and re-provisioned. Since you will probably not want to lose access to your domain while its host is offline, live migration looks really attractive.

The Xen hypervisor monitors real-time changes to the origin domain and forwards them to the destination along with the image itself. Once all the registers have been loaded on the new host, the new (target) domain is started. If the load on the origin domain is too heavy, Xen may simply abort the migration.

To make live migration work, both the source and target servers should be running similar resources (block devices, etc.), CPUs from the same family and should have access to shared storage, file systems paths should match, and both domains should be attached to identically-named network bridges. You will also need sufficient bandwidth and access to your storage device (make sure that **PermitRootLogin** in the target's **/etc/ssh/sshd_config** file is set to "yes"). The actual migration requires only the **xl migrate** command, the name of the domain to be moved, and the path to the new host:

```
# xl migrate <domain> <host>
```

If you don't have any available built-in shared storage accessible to both your source and target machines, running nbd-client allows you to share a storage device between hosts as long as both hosts remain up.

NBD (Network Block Device) is a protocol that lets you present a networked block device (such as a hard disk, a floppy, or a CD-ROM) for use on a local system. This expands the ways you can access your data, but it can also add migration options.

To use NBD in a migration, install ndb-client on the Dom0 you'd like to share your drive with, and ndb-server on the Dom0 that owns the drive. Add these lines to the **/etc/nbd-server/config** file on the drive host Dom0 (assuming sda1 is the drive you need to share):

```
[<name>]
    exportname = /dev/sda1
    port = 9000
```

Now, run **nbd-client** on the target machine:

```
nbd-client hostname-of-source 9000 /dev/nbd1
```

...And edit the **/etc/xen/VMname.cfg** file on the source host to use **/dev/nbd1** as its disk. Finally, run

```
# xl migrate <Domain> <new host>
```

...and you're ready to go.

Resources:	
Project Home:	xenproject.org
Documentation:	xenproject.org/help/documentation.html
Getting Started:	xenproject.org/users/getting-started.html
Wiki:	wiki.xen.org/wiki/Xen_Project_Software_Overview
SPICE:	wiki.xenproject.org/wiki/SPICE_support_in_Xen

Command Cheat Sheet

Build PV guest image	xen-create-image
Launch PV guest domain	xl create -c /etc/xen/myNewGuest.cfg
Open new console session	xl console <domain-id>
Close console	CTRL-]
Remove CDRom (within domain)	eject
Listen for new CDRom	eject -t
List domains	xl list
Display info	xl info
Display boot info	xl dmesg
Shutdown domain	xl shutdown <domain ID>
Destroy domain	xl destroy <domain ID>
Create HVM domain	xl create /etc/xen/ubuntu-hvm.cfg
List blocks by domain	xl block-list <domain-id>
Attach a new block	xl block-attach <domain-id> /dev/vg/guest-volume,,hda
Detach a block	xl block-detach <domain-id> <device-id>
List network	xl network-list <domain-id>
Attach network	xl network-attach <domain-id> <device>
Detach network	xl network-detach <domain-id> /local/domain/0 /backend/vif/1/0
Set a domain's vCPU count	xl vcpu-set 1 2
Migrate a domain	xl migrate <domain-id> <host>
Start a VM	xe vm-start vm=<VM name>

List VMs	xe vm-list
List remove VMs	xe -s 10.0.0.3 -u ubuntu -pw mypassword vm-list
List available networks	xe network-list
Create new network	xe network-create name-label=<mynetwork name>
Designate virtual CDRom	xe vm-cd-add cd-name=MyVirtualCD vm=My VMName device=/dev/sda
Restart	xe-toolstack-restart
Destroy VM	xe vm-destroy uuid=<UUID>
List disks	xe vm-disk-list vm=<vm name>
Resize a disk	xe vdi-resize uuid=<vdi uuid> size=<size>
Monitoring	xentop
List xenstore data	xenstore-ls
Test for xenstore key	xenstore-exists <keyname>
Read xenstore key value	xenstore-read <keyname>
Remove xenstore key	xenstore-rm <keyname>

Test Yourself

1. In Xen terminology, which of these best describes the basic function of Dom0:

a) It is the first guest domain

b) It is the hypervisor

c) It manages other domains

d) It is the last guest domain

2. Which of these tools will help you set up networking for your Xen environment?

a) lvm2

b) bridge-utils

c) xen-hypervisor-amd64

d) pvcreate

3. What resources does the /usr/share/xen-tools directory contain?

a) Scripts for building distribution images

b) Xen resource files

c) binary files for use within the Xen usespace

d) sample configuration files

4. To which directory should you save your image .cfg configuration files?

a) /etc/networking

b) /etc/sysconfig

c) /var/lib/xen

d) /etc/xen

5. Which of the following is NOT primarily a monitoring tool?

a) xentop

b) xl dmesg

c) vncviewer

d) xe vm-list

Answer Key: 1:c, 2:b,3:a,4:d,5:c

3. KVM

LPIC-304 Exam Objective 330.3

What is KVM?

Installation

KVM Management Tools

What is KVM?

Like Xen, KVM (Kernel-based Virtual Machine) is an open source hypervisor technology for virtualizing compute infrastructure running on x86 compatible hardware. Also like Xen, KVM has both an active user community and significant enterprise deployments.

A KVM host actually runs on the Linux kernel along with two KVM kernel modules (the kvm.ko module and either kvm-intel.ko or kvm-amd.ko). Through its tight kernel integration - including the I/O connectivity with kernel block and network drivers provided by Virtio - KVM can offer its guests more seamless access to all the complex hardware and networking profiles that they might encounter.

Hardware virtualization extensions built into modern CPU designs and required for KVM deployments mean that, right out of the box, KVM guests can safely access only those hardware resources they need without the need to worry about leakage to the larger system.

Where exactly does QEMU fit in with all this? Besides being able to act as a hypervisor, QEMU's strength is as an emulator. KVM, in its hypervisor virtualization role, can tap on to QEMU's emulation powers to compliment its own hardware acceleration features, presenting its guests with an emulated chipset and PCI bus. The whole, as they say, can be greater than the sum of its parts.

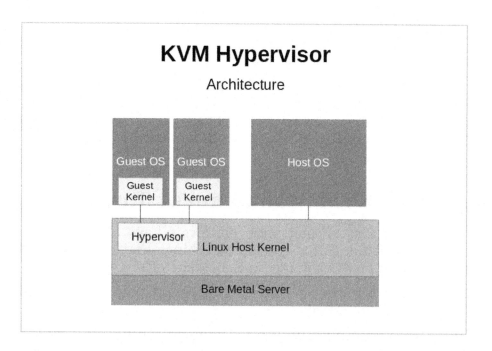

A great deal of management functionality for KVM is often actually provided by Libvirt. Therefore, you might sometimes want to refer to the detailed information about KVM-related features like networking, storage, and file system layouts that's found in Chapter Five ("Libvirt and Related Tools").

Installation

Before anything else, you'll need to make sure that the physical machine you're planning to use as a KVM host supports hardware virtualization. Besides the BIOS setting and the contents of **/proc/cpuinfo** (which we discussed in Chapter One), you can also quickly check this from a running Linux system using kvm-ok:

```
$ kvm-ok
```

It's also a good idea to be sure which hardware architecture - 64 or 32-bit - you're working with:

```
$ uname -m
```

But even if your hardware profile is up to the task, you'll have to let the Linux kernel in on your plans. If they're not already there, you should add the kvm and either kvm-intel or kvm-amd kernel modules.

```
# modprobe kvm
# modprobe kvm-intel
```

If those modules fail to load (and there's no /dev/kvm device in the file system), then there's a good chance your CPU just isn't up to the job you'd like it to to. However, if all that worked out, you're ready to install the **qemu-kvm** package (and, if necessary, **libvirt**, **virt-install**, and **bridge-utils** as well).

Working with KVM Management Tools

It's no secret that virtualization platforms have a well-deserved reputation for being complicated. But there are two things that can make getting started with KVM just a bit more challenging than some of the others:

- There are quite a few management toolkits available, each offering similar - but not identical - functionality.

- They have a nasty habit of changing the names used for the key binaries depending on which distribution and release you're using.

I'll introduce you to **Libvirt Tools** and **vmbuilder** in Chapter Five, but here, we'll discuss the **KVM** tool kit.

KVM

Building new guests using what we'll call the "KVM" way is a two step process. First, you'll use qemu-img to create a new image - or modify or convert an old one. Then you'll use qemu-kvm to set up a virtual machine that will start up the installation.

> *Did I just say "you'll use qemu-kvm..."? Silly me. qemu-kvm was merged into qemu a long time ago and has been replaced by qemu-system-x86_64. In the meantime, some systems offer you kvm as a wrapper that executes qemu-system-x86_64 -enable-kvm - although you shouldn't confuse the kvm wrapper with the old kvm binary that used a somewhat different syntax.*

So let's see how these two steps work. You create a disk image with **qemu-img** (which, by the way, can be used very effectively for other hypervisors as well), where "my-disk" is the name of the image you'd like to create, the maximum size of the image will be 6 GB, and qcow2 is the file format. qcow, by the way, stands for "QEMU Copy On Write".

```
# qemu-img create -f qcow2 /home/username/myimages/my-disk.img 6G
Formatting       '/home/username/myimages/my-disk.img',       fmt=qcow2
size=6442450944        encryption=off        cluster_size=65536
lazy_refcounts=off refcount_bits=16
#
```

> *Choosing a file format will depend on your sepcific needs. If you need greater compatibility and flexibility - including the ability to generate sophisticated snapshots - then qcow2 is probably going to be your best choice.*
>
> *The qcow disk image format permits disk space allocation to grow only as needed, meaning the use of space is always as efficient as possible. Changes to a qcow read-only image can be saved to a separate file, which refers internally to the original image. qcow2 added the ability to create multiple image snapshots.*

We're now ready for step two. Here's how we'll build our VM:

```
#   kvm   -name   my-VM   -hda   /home/username/myimages/my-disk.img
-cdrom /home/username/Downloads/ubuntu-16.04-server-amd64.iso -boot
d -m 1024
#
```

A new SDL window will often (although not necessarily for all distributions) pop up where you can complete the operating system installation process. Regaining control of your mouse from the Qemu terminal requires pressing **CTRL+ALT**.

To explain: using "**kvm**" (although the precise command you'll need for your version may differ), we'll call our new guest "my-VM", designate the my-disk.img file as hda ("hard drive a"), point to the location of the operating system ISO (Ubuntu 16.04 server, in this case), and set 1024 MB as the maximum memory alloted to the VM.

By default, KVM will configure your guest for user-level networking (as though the parameters **-netdev user,id=user.0 -device e1000,netdev=user.0** were specified). This will provide the guest with an IP address through KVM's own DHCP service and access to your host, the Internet, and to LAN-based recourses. While the default configuration is simple, it may be overly restrictive for some scenarios, as there are often some performance and feature limitations.

Besides these, you can use command line flags to control various VM configuration parameters, including:

- **-smp 2** provides two processors ("smp" = symmetric multiprocessing).

- The **-net** argument (example: -net nic,model=virtio,macaddr =52:54:00:05:11:11) establishes a network connection for your guest.

- You can provision a network bridge using something like **-net bridge,vlan=0,br=br0** - although this will require a matching -net definition on the host. The two are connected through a special "vlan" parameter.

- **-balloon virtio** will allow me to expand or reduce a guest's memory size without having to reboot it.

- You can also use the **-drive file=** flag to define additional block storage devices. Adding a value for **format=** (qcow2, for instance).

The **-M** flag will assign a specific machine type hardware emulation. **pc**. For example, will provide a standard PC profile. For a complete list of available machine types, you can run **kvm -M ?**:

```
$ kvm -M ?
Supported machines are:
ubuntu                   Ubuntu 15.04 PC (i440FX + PIIX, 1996) (alias
of pc-i440fx-wily)
pc-i440fx-wily     Ubuntu 15.04 PC (i440FX + PIIX, 1996) (default)
ubuntu          Ubuntu 15.04 PC (i440FX + PIIX, 1996) (alias of pc-
i440fx-vivid)
pc-i440fx-vivid    Ubuntu 15.04 PC (i440FX + PIIX, 1996) (default)
pc-i440fx-utopic   Ubuntu 14.10 PC (i440FX + PIIX, 1996)
pc-i440fx-trusty   Ubuntu 14.04 PC (i440FX + PIIX, 1996)
pc         Standard PC (i440FX + PIIX, 1996) (alias of pc-i440fx-2.5)
pc-i440fx-2.5      Standard PC (i440FX + PIIX, 1996)
pc-i440fx-2.4      Standard PC (i440FX + PIIX, 1996)
pc-i440fx-2.3      Standard PC (i440FX + PIIX, 1996)
pc-i440fx-2.2      Standard PC (i440FX + PIIX, 1996)
pc-i440fx-2.1      Standard PC (i440FX + PIIX, 1996)
pc-i440fx-2.0      Standard PC (i440FX + PIIX, 1996)
pc-i440fx-1.7      Standard PC (i440FX + PIIX, 1996)
pc-i440fx-1.6      Standard PC (i440FX + PIIX, 1996)
pc-i440fx-1.5      Standard PC (i440FX + PIIX, 1996)
pc-i440fx-1.4      Standard PC (i440FX + PIIX, 1996)
pc-1.3             Standard PC (i440FX + PIIX, 1996)
pc-1.2             Standard PC (i440FX + PIIX, 1996)
pc-1.1             Standard PC (i440FX + PIIX, 1996)
pc-1.0             Standard PC (i440FX + PIIX, 1996)
pc-0.15            Standard PC (i440FX + PIIX, 1996)
pc-0.14            Standard PC (i440FX + PIIX, 1996)
pc-0.13            Standard PC (i440FX + PIIX, 1996)
pc-0.12            Standard PC (i440FX + PIIX, 1996)
pc-0.11            Standard PC (i440FX + PIIX, 1996)
pc-0.10            Standard PC (i440FX + PIIX, 1996)
q35                Standard PC (Q35 + ICH9, 2009) (alias of pc-
q35-2.5)
pc-q35-2.5         Standard PC (Q35 + ICH9, 2009)
pc-q35-2.4         Standard PC (Q35 + ICH9, 2009)
pc-q35-2.3         Standard PC (Q35 + ICH9, 2009)
pc-q35-2.2         Standard PC (Q35 + ICH9, 2009)
pc-q35-2.1         Standard PC (Q35 + ICH9, 2009)
pc-q35-2.0         Standard PC (Q35 + ICH9, 2009)
pc-q35-1.7         Standard PC (Q35 + ICH9, 2009)
pc-q35-1.6         Standard PC (Q35 + ICH9, 2009)
pc-q35-1.5         Standard PC (Q35 + ICH9, 2009)
pc-q35-1.4         Standard PC (Q35 + ICH9, 2009)
isapc              ISA-only PC
none               empty machine
xenfv              Xen Fully-virtualized PC
xenpv              Xen Para-virtualized PC
$
```

KVM Monitor

While working with QEMU, you can open a monitor console and interact with your clients in ways that might be difficult or even impossible using a regular headless server. You can launch the KVM Monitor by pressing **CTRL+ALT**, and then **SHIFT+2**, and a new console will open on your desktop. **SHIFT+1** will close the console. You can also access the console from the command line using something like:

```
$ kvm -monitor stdio
```

You will probably NOT be able to launch the monitor as root (i.e., via sudo). Naturally, your version may require "**qemu-system-x86_64**" rather than kvm. This approach allows you to add command line arguments (like that **-monitor** which specified a console target). Consult **man qemu-system-x86_64** for details on the kinds of operations the monitor allows.

This example (borrowed from en.wikibooks.org/wiki/QEMU/Monitor) will list all the block devices currently available to your system, and then point one of them to an ISO file you want to use:

```
(qemu) info block
ide0-hd0: type=hd removable=0 file=/path/to/winxp.img
ide0-hd1: type=hd removable=0 file=/path/to/pagefile.raw
ide1-hd1: type=hd removable=0 file=/path/to/testing_data.img
ide1-cd0:  type=cdrom  removable=1  locked=0  file=/dev/sr0  ro=1
drv=host_device
floppy0: type=floppy removable=1 locked=0 [not inserted]
sd0: type=floppy removable=1 locked=0 [not inserted]
(qemu) change ide1-cd0 /home/images/my.iso
```

Networking

By default, a KVM guest will receive an IP address within the 10.0.2.0/24 subnet, and have outgoing access (including SSH access) both to its host, and to the wider network beyond. By that same default however, it won't be able to *host* services for network clients. If you need to open up incoming network connectivity, you'll probably want to create a network bridge on your host that's similar to the one we used for Xen in the previous chapter. As before, you will install **bridge-utils** on the host and, assuming you're running a Debian-based system and you want your host to receive its IP from a network DHCP server, edit the **/etc/network/interfaces** to look something like this (on CentOS machines, edit files in the **/etc/sysconfig/network-scripts/** directory):

```
auto lo
iface lo inet loopback

auto eth0
iface eth0 inet manual

auto br0
iface br0 inet dhcp
        bridge_ports eth0
        bridge_stp off
        bridge_fd 0
        bridge_maxwait 0
```

On CentOS, you'll need to create an ifcfg-br0 file in the **/etc/sysconfig/network-scripts/** directory to look something like this:

```
DEVICE=br0
TYPE=Bridge
BOOTPROTO=static
DNS1=192.168.0.1
GATEWAY=192.168.0.1
IPADDR=192.168.0.100
NETMASK=255.255.255.0
ONBOOT=yes
SEARCH="example.com"
```

...And then add a line reading **BRIDGE=br0** line to your primary network interface file (which will often be: **/etc/sysconfig/network-scripts/ifcfg-eth0**).

You will then stop and restart your network services (or reboot).

Resources:	
Project Home:	linux-kvm.org/page/Main_Page
Documentation:	linux-kvm.org/page/Documents

Command Cheat Sheet

Check for KVM support	kvm-ok
Check hardware architecture	uname -m
Add KVM modules	modprobe kvm
	modprobe kvm-intel
	modprobe kvm-amd
Create KVM disk image	qemu-img create [...]
Build a VM	kvm -name my-VM [...]
List supported machine types	kvm -M ?
Access console	kvm -monitor stdio

Test Yourself

1. Which of these statements is most correct?

a) QEMU is an emulator that allows PV VMs while KVM's strength is hardware acceleration

b) QEMU is an emulator that allows HVM VMs while KVM's strength is hardware acceleration

c) KVM allows both PV and HVM VMs, while QEMU allows only HVM

d) The two cannot be used together

2. What does the -M flag point to when used with kvm?

a) Machine type

b) Maximum memory

c) Minimum memory

d) Media source drive

Answer Key: 1:b,2:a

4. Other Virtualization Solutions

LPIC-304 Exam Objective 330.4

LXC

OpenVZ

Docker

VirtualBox

Packer

Vagrant

Containers

Not every virtual compute job is a good candidate for a full virtualization solution like Xen. Because Xen-like hypervisors use full hardware virtualization, they require a lot of space and system resources to function. Containers, on the other hand, provide virtualization of a very different sort by sharing their host's Linux kernel and all of its resources, potentially allowing you to pack many times more containers on to a single bare-metal server than you could using a hypervisor architecture.

Since containers share the kernel of their host, it's critically important to carefully define exactly which system resources containers will have access to and which will be off-limits. Tools like **Namespaces** provide abstracted file systems and resource visibility and **cgroups** control resource and process isolation. Kernel operations like **modprobe** will not work from within a container, but modules loaded on the host will be available to containers.

One critical ingredient of Google's secret sauce has been their heavy reliance on containers, which they create in response to individual

LXC

One very popular container technology is LXC - which stands for LinuX Containers. LXC uses namespaces to sandbox individual containers, allowing them controlled access to system resources, but through the abstraction of unique virtual filesystems. Thus, for example, users within one container will be able to view and manage their own processes running locally, but will have no access to processes belonging to other containers or to the host itself.

Because they're all sharing a single kernel, of course, you can't launch an LXC container running a different operating system than that of the host - that kind of versatility would require a hypervisor. However, any Linux distribution running your kernel release (based on the same CPU architecture) can, in theory at least, be run.

On Debian-based systems, you simply install the **lxc** package on your host and, without the need for any changes to your kernel, you're all ready to get started. Things are just a bit more complicated for CentOS/RHEL users. You will first need to install the EPEL repositories, then the Perl and debootstrap packages, and finally LXC itself and its templates.

```
# yum install epel-release
# yum install debootstrap perl libvirt
# yum install lxc lxc-templates
```

While it is possible to configure LXC to be accessible to even unprivileged users, by default you'll need root authority to work with the LXC filesystem. **lxc-ls --fancy** will display all the containers that currently exist on your system...whether or not they're running.

```
# lxc-ls --fancy
```

To create a new container, use **lxc-create**, specifying a template (ubuntu, in this case), and a container name.

```
# lxc-create -t ubuntu -n myname
```

You will find scripts for various templates in either **/usr/share/lxc/templates/** or **/usr/share/lxc/** (depending on your particular distribution). Here's the output from Ubuntu 16.04:

```
$ ls /usr/share/lxc/templates
lxc-alpine          lxc-centos          lxc-fedora      lxc-oracle
lxc-ubuntu-cloud    lxc-altlinux        lxc-cirros      lxc-gentoo
lxc-plamo           lxc-archlinux       lxc-debian
lxc-openmandriva    lxc-sshd            lxc-busybox     lxc-download
lxc-opensuse        lxc-ubuntu
$
```

Since the LXC containers are built from simple templates that reference the host kernel rather than complete and independent OS images or .iso files, they will often lack some of the "bells and whistles" features that you might normally expect. You might therefore need to add extra resources and packages to support templates from outside your own distribution ecosystem. Building a CentOS container on a Debian host, for example, might require that you install the Yum package manager on the non-CentOS host itself:

```
# apt install yum
```

Login information should be displayed at the end of the container creation process. By default, Ubuntu LXCs use "ubuntu" for both the username and password. CentOS will keep a temporary password for the root user in a file called **/var/lib/lxc/my-centos/tmp_root_pass** (which, of course, will be accessible from the host when using admin privileges). In any case, you might want to consider updating your password once you log in for the first time.

Assuming that you named your new container "my-lxc", its filesystem and configuration files will, by default, all be found in **/var/lib/lxc/my-lxc/**. You will need to be root to access the files.

```
$ sudo su
# cd /var/lib/lxc/MyContainerName
```

The my-lxc directory will contain a "config" file that defines your container's basic settings, a special "fstab" file that can be used for mounting drives within your container, and a directory called "rootfs". This directory contains the actual container filesystem and is a great place to perform system administration tasks from outside the container itself - even when it's not running.

Once installation is complete, you launch your new container using **lxc-start**:

```
# lxc-start -d -n MyContainerName
```

You'll probably want to use -d to detach from the new session, as otherwise, the only way to exit your shell will be to shut down the container.

You log in to a running LXC container either using a regular ssh connection, or through the console command:

```
# lxc-console -n MyContainerName
```

Getting out of the LXC shell can be a challenge if no one's told you the secret: after closing your container session using exit, you will need to hit CTRL+a and then q.

Your containers will probably be given IP addresses on the 10.0.3.0 subnet and will have access to other containers and the host itself through a network bridge (probably named lxcbr0) installed on the host. Here's how the bridge will appear from the host:

```
$ ip addr show dev lxcbr0
4: lxcbr0: <BROADCAST,MULTICAST,UP,LOWER_UP> mtu 1500 qdisc noqueue
state UP group default
    link/ether fe:74:13:f4:4d:8a brd ff:ff:ff:ff:ff:ff
    inet 10.0.3.1/24 brd 10.0.3.255 scope global lxcbr0
      valid_lft forever preferred_lft forever
    inet6 fe80::547d:9bff:fe81:55fa/64 scope link
      valid_lft forever preferred_lft forever
$ brctl show lxcbr0
bridge       name bridge id   STP enabled    interfaces
lxcbr0       8000.fe7413f44d8a     no         vethA9HGCX
```

And here's how it will appear from within the container:

```
$ ip addr show
1: lo: <LOOPBACK,UP,LOWER_UP> mtu 65536 qdisc noqueue state UNKNOWN
group default
    link/loopback 00:00:00:00:00:00 brd 00:00:00:00:00:00
    inet 127.0.0.1/8 scope host lo
      valid_lft forever preferred_lft forever
    inet6 ::1/128 scope host
      valid_lft forever preferred_lft forever
5:  eth0@if6:  <BROADCAST,MULTICAST,UP,LOWER_UP>  mtu  1500   qdisc
pfifo_fast state UP group default qlen 1000
    link/ether 00:16:3e:0c:18:d2 brd ff:ff:ff:ff:ff:ff
    inet 10.0.3.234/24 brd 10.0.3.255 scope global eth0
      valid_lft forever preferred_lft forever
    inet6 fe80::216:3eff:fe0c:18d2/64 scope link
      valid_lft forever preferred_lft forever
$
```

Resources:	
Project Home:	linuxcontainers.org
Documentation:	linuxcontainers.org/lxc/manpages/
Getting Started:	linuxcontainers.org/lxc/getting-started/

OpenVZ

Another container technology - which some think of as a precursor to LXC - is OpenVZ. OpenVZ is described as "the basis" of the commercial container virtualization product **Virtuozzo** which, while currently marketed under the Odin brand, is still more popularly associated with the Parallels name.

While OpenVZ shares the host OS and uses a namespace environment just like LXC, it requires a specially patched Linux kernel to run with all its features and isn't quite so simple to deploy.

Using OpenVZ on Debian-based systems is a difficult process. For that reason, I'll show you how to get it running on CentOS 6. To install OpenVZ, you'll need to add the OpenVZ repository to your system. Use wget like this:

```
$ wget -P /etc/yum.repos.d/ http://ftp.openvz.org/openvz.repo
```

You then import the OpenVZ key for signing RPM packages:

```
# rpm --import http://ftp.openvz.org/RPM-GPG-Key-OpenVZ
```

Finally, you install the package and its tools through yum:

```
# yum install vzkernel vzctl vzquota ploop
```

Once you reboot your system, OpenVZ should be running. Before you can actually launch your first container, however, you'll need to add at least one OS template to the **/vz/template/cache/** directory.

```
$ cd /vz/template/cache
$ wget http://download.openvz.org/template/precreated/centos-5-x86_64.tar.gz
```

To create a container running CentOS called 101 (since OpenVZ has reserved the first 100 numbers for future use, you should avoid using numbers lower than 101), you would run **vzctl create**:

```
# vzctl create 101 --ostemplate centos-5-x86 --config basic
```

You can use vzctl to manage system configuration for your containers. If, for instance, you'd like to give your container a static IP address, you can use **vzctl --ipadd**. **--save** tells vzctl to save the setting to the configuration file.

```
# vzctl set 101 --ipadd 10.0.4.25 --save
```

vzctl controls your container's run state. This command will launch the container that had been given the container ID of 101:

```
# vzctl start 101
```

vzctl can control processes on a running container from the host machine through exec. Running:

```
# vzctl exec 101 apachectl start
```

...for instance, will start the Apache web server service on a virtual machine running systemd.

And, since you're definitely going to want to enjoy shell sessions within your containers, you can open a new session using vzctl with the enter command:

```
# vzctl enter 101
```

Once the container is no longer needed, **vzctl stop** will shut it down, and **vzctl destroy** will delete it.

```
# vzctl stop 101
# vzctl destroy 101
```

One significant advantage of OpenVZ is its ability to generate a complete image of a working operating system - a process called checkpointing - which can then be used to precisely restore or create cloned copies. OpenVZ's live migration feature allows a running container to be moved from one server to another, complete with its network connections.

Besides LXC and OpenVZ, the **Linux Vserver** project also offers isolated containers, but hasn't been particularly popular over the past years and seems not to have been well maintained.

Resources:	
Project Home:	openvz.org/Main_Page
Documentation:	openvz.org/Category:HOWTO

Docker

While it doesn't play a huge role in the LPIC-3 304 exam, Docker is a container platform that's just too big to completely ignore. Originally built on top of the LXC engine (and later ported to their own libcontainer), Docker allows for super-light containers that are defined by scripts called Dockerfiles. In fact, of the millions of Docker containers that are regularly launched in all kinds of environments, I suspect that very few will ever host user shell sessions of any kind. Rather, they're far more likely to be controlled entirely by their Dockerfiles or from the command line of their hosts.

Docker containers have become a very popular tool for sharing development environments and reliably moving them between deployment stages. If you're familiar with either LXC or OpenVZ, then you won't have any trouble getting up to speed with the syntax used in Dockerfiles or Docker's command line. In fact, when I first encountered Docker a couple of years ago, I remember being surprised at how quickly it was all making sense to me...until the LXC connection became obvious.

Resources:	
Project Home:	docker.com
Documentation:	docs.docker.com
What is it?	docker.com/what-docker

VirtualBox and Vmware Player

As much as we might prefer the speed and power of the command line, sometimes there's no alternative to a GUI OS desktop interface. Oracle's VirtualBox and VMWare's Player are two free tools for running versions of a wide range of operating systems (including Windows and, in some cases, even Mac OS X) as virtual desktops on a Linux machine. Having said all that, VirtualBox does also come with a command line tool. See **man virtualbox** for details.

Besides the more obvious and straightforward uses for VirtualBox and Vmware Player to allow access to, say, Windows applications on a Linux machine, it's not uncommon to use them to simulate all kinds of complex, nested layers of virtualization involving multiple operating systems.

VirtualBox can load images based on a number of formats, including .ISO files, VMDK disk images, and an OVA (Open Virtual Appliance) package defined by an .XML-based Open Virtualization Format (OVF) file.

As we'll soon see, VirtualBox has also become the primary foundation of the Vagrant virtualization wrapper.

Resources:	
Project Home:	virtualbox.org
Documentation:	virtualbox.org/wiki/Documentation

Provisioning Tools

The HashiCorp company provides a suite of (mostly) free and open source virtual server provisioning tools. One of the strengths of these tools is their ability to provision a single image (or "artifact" in Packer terms) and deploy it as containers (or "boxes" as Vagrant describes them) over multiple providers. This way, you can precisely define an operating system environment (including the software packages you'd like installed) and have it reliably run for different purposes. You can also host Vagrant files in git-like repositories, allowing your team to pull identical environments with a single command.

You might want to have the development team run it locally on VirtualBox in complete isolation, let a remote team test it over and over again within their own LXC environment, and then move it to production on a cloud provider like AWS. Not only can you be sure that all your teams are seeing the exact same image, but any changes you commit to one iteration are automatically picked up in the others.

Packer

You can have Vagrant produce boxes based on a number of sources, but HashiCorp recommends building them in Packer. You can install Packer by downloading and then unzipping the latest archive into a new directory - I'm using **/usr/local/packer/**.

```
$ wget
https://releases.hashicorp.com/packer/0.8.6/packer_0.8.6_linux_amd6
4.zip
$ unzip packer_0.8.6_linux_amd64.zip
```

This will give you a packer binary and three kinds of scripts that can be called from your Packer template: **builders** (to generate machine images meant to run on a specific platform like VirtualBox, AWS, or Docker), **provisioners** (to configure software and system settings for a running image before it's generated), and **post processors** (to generate artifacts out of the builders' images).

```
ubuntu@localhost:/usr/local/packer$ ls
packer                                packer-post-processor-docker-
import
packer-builder-amazon-chroot          packer-post-processor-docker-push
packer-builder-amazon-ebs             packer-post-processor-docker-save
packer-builder-amazon-instance        packer-post-processor-docker-tag
packer-builder-digitalocean           packer-post-processor-vagrant
packer-builder-docker                 packer-post-processor-vagrant-
cloud
packer-builder-file                   packer-post-processor-vsphere
packer-builder-googlecompute          packer-provisioner-ansible-local
packer-builder-null                   packer-provisioner-chef-client
packer-builder-openstack              packer-provisioner-chef-solo
packer-builder-parallels-iso              packer-provisioner-file
packer-builder-parallels-pvm              packer-provisioner-
powershell
packer-builder-qemu                   packer-provisioner-puppet-
masterless
packer-builder-virtualbox-iso             packer-provisioner-puppet-
server
packer-builder-virtualbox-ovf         packer-provisioner-salt-masterless
packer-builder-vmware-iso             packer-provisioner-shell
packer-builder-vmware-vmx             packer-provisioner-shell-local
packer-post-processor-artifice        packer-provisioner-windows-restart
packer-post-processor-atlas           packer-provisioner-windows-shell
packer-post-processor-compress
$
```

All those components are brought together in a template.json file. Here's a very simple example (taken from Packer's own documentation pages: packer.io/intro/getting-started/build-image.html):

```
{
  "variables": {
    "aws_access_key": "",
    "aws_secret_key": ""
  },
  "builders": [{
    "type": "amazon-ebs",
    "access_key": "{{user `aws_access_key`}}",
    "secret_key": "{{user `aws_secret_key`}}",
    "region": "us-east-1",
    "source_ami": "ami-72b9e018",
    "instance_type": "t2.micro",
    "ssh_username": "ubuntu",
    "ami_name": "packer-example {{timestamp}}"
  }]
}
```

You could create a file with these contents called example.json. The template defines amazon-ebs as its builder and passes authentication and configuration information - including an AWS region, Amazon Machine Image (AMI) an instance type. You could either include your AWS keys in the template itself or pass them as variables from the command line.

You get Packer to build your artifacts using **packer build**:

```
# packer build example.json
```

The output of this command will be a usable image - an AWS AMI, in this case. Naturally, if your template included an image you'd like to manage in Vagrant, you could push it to Hashicorp's version control system, Atlas so Vagrant can get to work on it:

```
# packer push -name myAtlasName/mynewexample example2.json
```

Vagrant

Before you can install Vagrant, you have to decide which provider you want to use and make sure it's properly installed on your host system. As I mentioned above, the most common approach is to install Oracle's VirtualBox along with Vagrant. There are plenty of how-to guides online to help you through the set up process - although I suspect that there are also just as many discussion threads documenting frustrating conflicts between layers of the software stack.

To be complete, however, I'll quickly show you how to get a simple Vagrant box up and running using the standard VirtualBox configuration. Once you've installed both the **virtualbox** and **vagrant** packages, add a development environment using, for example, trusty64:

```
# vagrant init ubuntu/trusty64
A `Vagrantfile` has been placed in this directory. You are now
ready to `vagrant up` your first virtual environment! Please read
the comments in the Vagrantfile as well as documentation on
`vagrantup.com` for more information on using Vagrant.
#
```

Now, launch your new environment using vagrant up.

```
# vagrant up
Bringing machine 'default' up with 'virtualbox' provider...
==> default: Checking if box 'ubuntu/trusty64' is up to date...
#
```

Just to offer a different perspective, I will also illustrate setting up Vagrant to use LXC as its base. I'll assume that you're using Ubuntu 16.04 for this process.

We'll start by installing LXC itself (along with redir - for those planning to use port forwarding).

```
# apt install lxc lxc-templates cgroup-lite redir
```

It's a good idea to avoid the Vagrant package that's in the Debian repositories - especially when you're using older distribution releases - so I'll directly download and install the latest Vagrant release from their web site:

```
$ wget https://releases.hashicorp.com/vagrant/1.8.4/vagrant
_1.8.4_x86_64.deb
# dpkg -i vagrant_1.8.4_x86_64.deb
Selecting previously unselected package vagrant.
(Reading database ... 98318 files and directories currently
installed.)
Preparing to unpack vagrant_1.8.4_x86_64.deb ...
Unpacking vagrant (1:1.8.4) ...
Setting up vagrant (1:1.8.4) …
#
```

With Vagrant in, I'll use it to install our vagrant-lxc plugin:

```
# vagrant plugin install vagrant-lxc
```

Vagrant init will generate a Vagrantfile config file in the current directory. We'll point our init operation to an online project that was helpfully created by Fabio Rehm.

```
# vagrant init fgrehm/precise64-lxc
```

It's probably a good idea to take a look through the Vagrantfile to get an idea of how it works and how this particular project is built. One parameter that should interest you immediately is config.vm.box. By default, config.vm.box will be given the value "base", but our init operation wrote config as "fgrehm/precise64-lxc".

```
config.vm.box = "fgrehm/precise64-lxc"
```

Next, because there could be complications during the launch process revolving around root authentications, you might want to run **vagrant lxc sudoers**, which will create a script in your **/etc/sudoers.d/** directory effectively whitelisting LXC-related commands. As with all scripts you pick up from the Internet (or from technical books like this one, for that matter) you really must read them through carefully to make sure that they're not doing anything dangerous. It's your system so, ultimately, it's your responsibility.

```
# vagrant lxc sudoers
```

Finally, we're ready to launch our Vagrant project (or "box" as they're called in Vagrant circles). In this case, we'll point "up" to our LXC provider.

```
# vagrant up --provider=lxc
```

Now that you've got a box running, we can work with it from the command line using Vagrant. Run **vagrant** on its own for a quick list of commands. Among them, you will find **vagrant ssh**, which will open a secure shell so you can administrate the running container.

```
# vagrant ssh
```

But that kind of defeats the purpose of Vagrant, which is really all about scripting things so you don't have to manage them directly.

Vagrant lets you push boxes that you've configured to Atlas so others can access it. You would set the **Vagrantfile config.push.define** attribute with your Atlas user name and application name so Vagrant will know what to do with it. Atlas, by the way, is HashiCorp's enterprise platform.

```
# vagrant push
```

Vagrant status will return the status of the current running box, and **share** let's you share your environment with others.

```
# vagrant status
# vagrant share
```

You can add additional boxes to your Vagrant environment using **box add**. This command will download the trusty64 image from the Atlas box catalog. You could just as easily add local or shared images. This particular box, by the way, won't work with our LXC provider: it's actually built for VirtualBox.

```
# vagrant box add ubuntu/trusty64
```

Command Cheat Sheet

List LXC containers	lxc-ls --fancy
Create a container	lxc-create -t ubuntu -n myname
LXC templates	/usr/share/lxc/templates/
LXC file systems	/var/lib/lxc/
Start an LXC container	lxc-start -d -n myname
Login to LXC container	lxc-console -n myname
Create OpenVZ container	vzctl create 101 --ostemplate centos-5-x86 --config basic
Assign static IP	vzctl set 101 --ipadd 10.0.4.25 --save
Launch OpenVZ container	vzctl start 101
Control process	vzctl exec 101 apachectl start
Build Packer artifact	packer build example.json
Push image	packer push -name myAtlasName/mynewexample example2.json
Initialize Vagrant box	vagrant init ubuntu/trusty64
Launch Vagrant box	vagrant up
Open SSH session on box	vagrant ssh
Display status of box	vagrant status
Share an environment	vagrant share

Resources:	
Project Home:	packer.io, vagrantup.com
Getting Started:	vagrantup.com/docs/getting-started/
Documentation:	packer.io/docs/

Test Yourself

1. Which of the following technologies requires that a VM share its host's kernel?

a) LXC

b) Xen

c) VirtualBox

d) Vagrant

2. When creating a new LXC container, what role does the -t argument play?

a) It defines the total memory allowed to the container

b) It sets the container type

c) It identifies the container name

d) It points to the container template file

3. OpenVZ container ID names must...

a) be shorter than 64 characters

b) be higher than 100

c) contain only alpha-numeric characters

d) begin with OpenVZ

4. The OpenVZ command line tool is called...

a) vzsys

b) ovzcmd

c) vzctl

d) crm

5. Docker containers are defined by which of these:

a) dockerfiles

b) XML files

c) bash scripts

d) JSON formatted scripts

6. When using Vagrant's Packer, which of the following will generate artifacts?

a) builders

b) post processors

c) provisioners

d) boxes

Answer Key: 1:a,2:d,3:b,4:c,5:a, 6:b

5. Libvirt and Related Tools

LPIC-304 Exam Objective 330.5

Hypervisors
Libvirt Tools
vmbuilder
The virsh shell
Networking
Storage
oVirt
The API

In many ways, libvirt lies at the very heart of much of Linux virtualization. At its core, through its universal API and CLI, libvirt allows virtualization management tools to securely administrate domains through a common and reliable software layer. While it isn't a hypervisor or standalone platform on its own, it has pretty much become the de facto administration tool for KVM and can also be used to manage a number of virtualization technologies like XEN.

Libvirt provides three ways to interact with the infrastructure underlying your virtual resources:

- Hypervisor storage and network drivers
- The virsh command line shell (or GUI interfaces like oVirt)
- The API

Before I explain how each of those works, I should note that citizens of Libvirtland will sometimes describe things a little bit differently than you might expect. For the libvirt crowd, a "node" is a single physical machine that's used to host a hypervisor and virtual machines (VMs). A "hypervisor" is a software layer that can virtualize a node's resources as VMs running multiple operating systems. And a single instance of a VM is, for some reason, always referred to as a "domain".

One other introductory point: like so much else in Linux, all the fun stuff is in text files. The /etc/libvirt/ directory contains some basic system configuration files and scripts.

```
/etc/libvirt$ ls
hooks                  libvirtd.conf          nwfilter
qemu-lockd.conf        virt-login-shell.conf  libvirt.conf
lxc.conf qemu          qemu.conf              virtlockd.conf
/etc/libvirt$
```

Following an approach similar to other virtualization platforms, by default, the filesystems behind the domains live below the **/var/lib/libvirt/** directory.

If you don't need to compile your own build, you can install libvirt on a host node from standard repositories. For Debian-based systems, you'll need the **qemu-kvm**, **libvirt-bin**, and **virtinst** packages. For CentOS 7 and OpenSUSE (once you have the **Virtualization** repository added), **libvirt** alone is enough.

Hypervisors

Libvirt supports hypervisors through a driver architecture. That is, libvirt drivers written for specific hypervisor technologies will interpret API calls to present fully emulated hypervisor environments on which domain-based operating systems can launch.

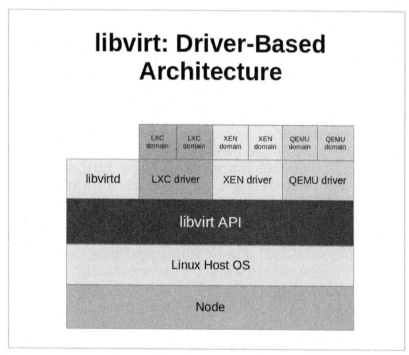

In Livbirt systems, resources used by domains are set by various XML files which define **storage volumes** (virtual disks or machine images), **storage pools** (partitions or file systems), **network devices** (like bridges and interfaces), and

snapshots: images saved within a volume representing an exact description of a domains' state.

Libvirt drivers currently exist for these environments (although they may not all run concurrently on a single host):

- Xen
- QEMU
- LXC
- OpenVZ
- UML (User Mode Linux)
- VirtualBox
- VMware ESX

- VMware Workstation/Player
- Microsoft Hyper-V
- IBM PowerVM (phyp)
- Virtuozzo
- Bhyve (the BSD hypervisor)
- Test (used for testing)

...and for these storage driver backends:

- Directory
- Local filesystem
- Network filesystem
- Logical Volume Manager (LVM)
- Disk

- iSCSI
- SCSI
- Multipath
- RBD (RADOS Block Device)
- Sheepdog

Libvirt Tools

Since both Xen and KVM can run on top of libvirt's libraries, libvirt's built-in management tools can directly perform many common hypervisor-related tasks. Installing the **libvirt-bin** package (on Debian/Ubuntu systems) will provide the **virsh** shell. For CentOS, it will already be part of the **libvirt** package, and openSUSE users will need to install **libvirt-client**.

Once you've got libvirt and a hypervisor platform up and running (with either Xen or KVM available), you can directly control your domains either from within the node itself or, assuming you've configured SSH access, remotely via the **libvirtd** daemon. There are a few ways to build a new guest domain: by defining your guest's parameters using **virt-install** (which can be installed through either the **virtinst** or **virt-install** package - depending on your distribution), copying the XML file of an existing domain through the **dumpxml** tool, or manually write your own XML file defining your guest's properties and then use the **virsh create** command. We'll start with virt-install.

The virsh Shell

Although Virsh commands can be run directly from the command line, it also has its own interactive shell that you access by simply typing **virsh**:

```
# virsh
Welcome to virsh, the virtualization interactive terminal.

Type:  'help' for help with commands
       'quit' to quit
virsh
virsh #
```

The Command Line

You can also do all your libvirt work - including creating a new domain - directly from the command line using **virt-install**, followed by your domain parameters, which will generate an XML file. To get things working, first make sure **Libvirt** is running and is set to load on boot:

```
# systemctl enable libvirtd
# systemctl start libvirtd
#    virt-install    -n    my_vm    -r    256    --vcpus=2    --disk
path=/var/lib/libvirt/images/web_devel.img,bus=virtio,size=1    -c
ubuntu-16.04-server-i386.iso --network network=default,model=virtio
--graphics vnc,listen=0.0.0.0 --noautoconsole -v
Starting install...
Allocating                                          'web_devel.img'
| 1.0 GB  00:00:00
Creating                                                  domain...
|   0 B  00:00:00
Domain installation still in progress. You can reconnect to
the console to complete the installation process.
#
```

Let's explain that one part at a time.

- **-n my_vm** sets the human-readable name for the new domain.
- **-r 256** declares the memory that will be available to the domain (in MB).
- **--vcpus=2** provisions two virtual CPUs.
- **--disk path=/var/lib/libvirt/images/my_vm.img** is the path to the virtual disk that will contain your image. **Size=1** sets the disk size to 1 GB (which, obviously will probably be a bit small for most uses).
- **-c ubuntu-14.04-server-i386.iso** points to the source iso file to be used as a virtual CDROM. You could also specify a real CDROM device on the host.
- **--network** tells us that the VM's default network will be used and configured for virtio.
- **--graphics vnc,listen=0.0.0.0:** allows VNC access through the host - this can be important, as you might need to log in remotely from a regular desktop PC to perform some administrative functions - or simply to complete your domain's operating system installation process - through a GUI interface.

virt-install has got the ball rolling, but you still have to log in through a graphic console of some sort to complete the installation process. Through our --graphics setting, we specified VNC as our console session, so open a VNC client on a machine, and point it to the hypervisor IP address (you might need to open your firewall to allow a VNC session).

The **virt-install** operation we just ran will create a file called my_vm.xml in the **/etc/libvirt/qemu/** directory that will look something like this:

```
<domain type='qemu'>
  <name>my_vm</name>
  <uuid>418f1471-c355-4531-9824-7021339bccd7</uuid>
  <memory unit='KiB'>262144</memory>
  <currentMemory unit='KiB'>262144</currentMemory>
  <vcpu placement='static'>2</vcpu>
  <os>
    <type arch='x86_64' machine='pc-i440fx-rhel7.0.0'>hvm</type>
    <boot dev='hd'/>
  </os>
  <features>
    <acpi/>
    <apic/>
  </features>
  <clock offset='utc'>
    <timer name='rtc' tickpolicy='catchup'/>
    <timer name='pit' tickpolicy='delay'/>
    <timer name='hpet' present='no'/>
  </clock>
  <on_poweroff>destroy</on_poweroff>
  <on_reboot>restart</on_reboot>
  <on_crash>restart</on_crash>
  <pm>
    <suspend-to-mem enabled='no'/>
    <suspend-to-disk enabled='no'/>
  </pm>
  <devices>
    <emulator>/usr/libexec/qemu-kvm</emulator>
    <disk type='file' device='disk'>
      <driver name='qemu' type='qcow2'/>
      <source file='/var/lib/libvirt/images/web_devel.img'/>
      <target dev='vda' bus='virtio'/>
        <address type='pci' domain='0x0000' bus='0x00' slot='0x04'
function='0x0'/>
    </disk>
    <disk type='block' device='cdrom'>
      <driver name='qemu' type='raw'/>
      <target dev='hda' bus='ide'/>
      <readonly/>
        <address type='drive' controller='0' bus='0' target='0'
unit='0'/>
    </disk>
    <controller type='usb' index='0' model='ich9-ehci1'>
        <address type='pci' domain='0x0000' bus='0x00' slot='0x05'
function='0x7'/>
    </controller>
    <controller type='usb' index='0' model='ich9-uhci1'>
      <master startport='0'/>
        <address type='pci' domain='0x0000' bus='0x00' slot='0x05'
function='0x0' multifunction='on'/>
```

```
        </controller>
        <controller type='usb' index='0' model='ich9-uhci2'>
          <master startport='2'/>
            <address type='pci' domain='0x0000' bus='0x00' slot='0x05'
function='0x1'/>
        </controller>
        <controller type='usb' index='0' model='ich9-uhci3'>
          <master startport='4'/>
            <address type='pci' domain='0x0000' bus='0x00' slot='0x05'
function='0x2'/>
        </controller>
        <controller type='pci' index='0' model='pci-root'/>
        <controller type='ide' index='0'>
            <address type='pci' domain='0x0000' bus='0x00' slot='0x01'
function='0x1'/>
        </controller>
        <interface type='network'>
          <mac address='52:54:00:af:58:b1'/>
          <source network='default'/>
          <model type='virtio'/>
            <address type='pci' domain='0x0000' bus='0x00' slot='0x03'
function='0x0'/>
      </interface>
      <serial type='pty'>
        <target port='0'/>
      </serial>
      <console type='pty'>
        <target type='serial' port='0'/>
      </console>
      <input type='mouse' bus='ps2'/>
      <input type='keyboard' bus='ps2'/>
      <graphics type='vnc' port='-1' autoport='yes' listen='0.0.0.0'>
        <listen type='address' address='0.0.0.0'/>
      </graphics>
      <video>
        <model type='cirrus' vram='16384' heads='1'/>
          <address type='pci' domain='0x0000' bus='0x00' slot='0x02'
function='0x0'/>
      </video>
      <memballoon model='virtio'>
          <address type='pci' domain='0x0000' bus='0x00' slot='0x06'
function='0x0'/>
      </memballoon>
    </devices>
</domain
```

You could also copy an existing domain using **dumpxml** and modify its contents
to suit your new needs:

```
# virsh dumpxml my_vm > new_vm.xml
# nano new_vm.xml
```

At the very least, you'll need to change the value of *<name>* and *<uuid>* before Virsh will start your new domain. Once you're confident that you've got the new XML file just the way you'd like it, you can create a new domain using **virsh create** like this:

```
# virsh create new_vm.xml
Domain new_vm created from new_vm.xml
#
```

create-as allows you to define the parameters for a new object, like this volume:

```
# virsh vol-create-as new_image_lvm volume1 2G
Vol volume1 created
#
```

Once you've got one or two live domains, you can list all the locally running domains with **list**.

```
# virsh list
 Id    Name                           State
----------------------------------------------------
 2     my_vm                          running
 3     new_vm                         running
#
```

With either the Domain ID that will be displayed or its name, you can interact with a domain. Thus, you can start a stopped domain this way:

```
# virsh start my_vm
```

You can similarly **stop** (the equivalent of an ACPI shutdown of a PC), **suspend** (meaning, the node will not accept scheduling from the hypervisor...although it will still consume system resources), **resume** (to wake up a node from its suspended state), or **destroy** a domain with syntax like this:

```
# virsh shutdown my_vm
```

You can edit the parameters of an XML file from an active domain, but never in the file itself. Rather, assuming that your domain is called "my_vm", you can use:

```
# virsh edit my_vm
```

There are similar virsh editing and backup tools for other libvirt XML configuration files:

1. **virsh net-edit default** will edit the XML settings for a specified network. It manages the **/etc/libvirt/qemu/networks/default.xml** file.
2. **virsh pool-edit home** edits the XML settings for a specified storage pool, acting on the **/etc/libvirt/storage/home.xml** file.
3. **virsh vol-dumpxml --pool home > newvol.xml** can create (and edit) a new volume from an existing pool.
4. **virsh iface-edit lo** can edit a specific network interface.

You can display the resources currently accessible (to know, for instance, where to point your virsh edit commands) using *-list commands:

```
# virsh net-list
 Name                 State      Autostart    Persistent
----------------------------------------------------------
 default              active     yes          yes
#
# virsh pool-list
 Name                 State      Autostart
---------------------------------------------
 home                 active     yes
 images               active     yes
#
# virsh vol-list --pool home
 Name                 Path
-----------------------------------------------------------------
 ubuntu-16.04-server-amd64.iso /home/ubuntu-16.04-server-amd64.iso
#
# virsh vol-list --pool images
 Name                 Path
-----------------------------------------------------------------
 web_devel.img        /var/lib/libvirt/images/web_devel.img
#
# virsh iface-list
 Name                 State      MAC Address
---------------------------------------------
 enp0s3               active     08:00:27:bb:21:8f
 lo                   active     00:00:00:00:00:00
#
```

You can connect to a local libvirtd instance using -c. Adding qemu:///system will log you in as root.

```
# virsh -c qemu:///system
```

Substituting "session" for "system" will log you in as a regular (non-root) user which, for security purposes, is sometimes preferred.

```
# virsh -c qemu:///session
```

qemu:/// is primarily used to provide virsh with absolute (and, when necessary, remote) addresses for the domains you're after. With that in mind, if you'd like to log in to a remote domain using ssh, you could use syntax like this:

```
# virsh -c qemu+ssh://root@hail.cloud.example.com/system
```

Don't blame me for the URI example: I took it from libvirt's own documentation. In any case, if all of that seems like a lot of typing, you could edit the /etc/libvirt/libvirt.conf file to create an alias. Here is the example from the comments included in that file:

```
uri_aliases = [
  "hail=qemu+ssh://root@hail.cloud.example.com/system",
  "sleet=qemu+ssh://root@sleet.cloud.example.com/system",
]
```

Finally, besides all kinds of useful online support information, typing **virsh help** will provide a rich collection of usage details:

```
# virsh help
```

Storage

KVM guests can exist quite happily using their own internal resources. Nevertheless, you might sometimes need some way to store and organize your disk images or to provide remote clients with access to them. You can define such resources and effectively mount them within a virtual machine by incorporating the contents of an XML file into your client's definition. This command tells the virsh tool "**pool-define**" to load the configuration found in a file called images_disk.xml in your **/etc/libvirt/storage/** directory:

```
# virsh pool-define ~/images_disk.xml
```

I'll briefly illustrate how such a file is formatted. Libvirt organizes storage resources as **pools**, dividing them into **volumes** that can be represented to a guest as **block devices**. So, for example, you could include a <pool> entry in your XML configuration of the "dir" type, that exposes the path to an image file on a local machine (example.com:/home/datauser/newfiles/) to the host system:

```
<pool type="dir">
   <name>virtimages</name>
   <target>
      <path>/var/lib/virt/images</path>
   </target>
</pool>
```

When not specified, Libvirt will use the default protocol of **auto**. The mounted data, once started from the host using **pool-start**...

```
# virsh pool-start
```

...will be accessible to the Libvirt API as volumes.

Besides the netfs (Network File System), other valid KVM/libvirt pool types include Directory (dir - as described above), iSCSI server (iSCSI), and Logical volume storage pool (Logical - as described below).

Assuming you've already defined an LVM volume group (called LVGName), this simple XML will define a logical volume pool.

```
<pool type="logical">
   <name>LVGName</name>
   <source>
     <device path="/dev/sda1"/>
     <device path="/dev/sdb1"/>
     <device path="/dev/sdc1"/>
   </source>
   <target>
     <path>/dev/LVGName</path>
   </target>
</pool>
```

Assuming the appropriate kernel modules are already loaded, you can add resources to a domain while it's running (or "hot" - hence the name "hotplugging").

```
modprobe acpiphp
modprobe pci_hotplug
```

Now, assuming that there's a new disk defined in the newdisk.xml file in your /etc/libvirt/storage/ directory, and your domain is called my_vm, you would add the disk using **virsh attach-device**:

```
# virsh attach-device my_vm /etc/libvirt/storage/newdisk.xml
```

Virtual Machine Manager

The virt-manager application is a simple GUI that lets you administrate KVM and Xen VMs, and LXC containers. Besides displaying status and performance information about your domains, it also provides wizards to configuring and creating new domains, and activates domain console sessions. The manager is available from repositories on all major Linux distributions as **virt-manager**, and is launched from the command line using **virt-manager**.

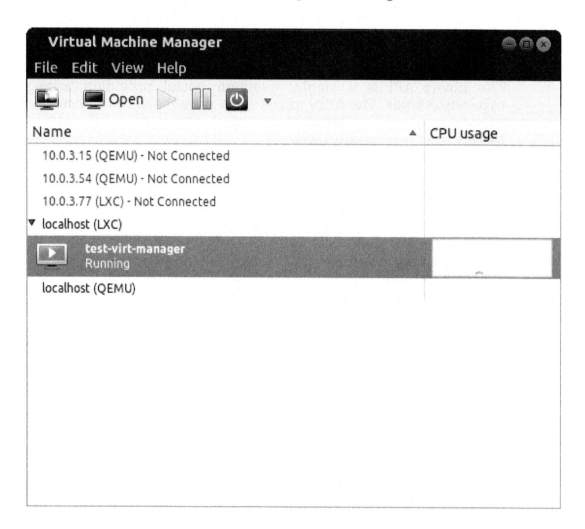

oVirt

You can administrate local or remote libvirt hypervisors through a web browser or Android mobile client using Red Hat Enterprise Virtualization's oVirt (or the moVirt app for Android). At this point, while the oVirt web site does offer manual guidance for Debian/Ubuntu installation, only relatively recent releases of Red Hat, CentOS, Fedora, and Scientific Linux are fully supported as hosts. You can, of course, use oVirt to orchestrate the full range of virtualized resources a very wide range of guest VMs.

To be useful, oVirt will need at least one running host node: they recommend using either Fedora, CentOS or their own oVirt Node.

While oVirt is well documented, I will observe that the "Quick" Start Guide on their web site contains more than 9000 words - which does suggest a rather high level of complexity.

oVirt includes tools for automating clustering and load balancing, and has a broader range of features than **virt-manager**.

The API

The libvirt API is a single, common portal providing access to all libvirt hypervisor types. The API's universality does mean that there are some platform-specific features that are not supported. Those, obviously, can be administrated by way of alternate interfaces.

Here's a Python snippet including an API call:

```
import libvirt
conn = libvirt.open('qemu:///system')
for id in conn.listDomainsID():
    dom = conn.lookupByID(id)
    print "Dom %s  State %s" % ( dom.name(), dom.info()[0] )
    dom.suspend()
    print "Dom %s   State %s (after suspend)" % ( dom.name(),
dom.info()[0] )
    dom.resume()
    print "Dom %s   State %s (after resume)" % ( dom.name(),
dom.info()[0] )
    dom.destroy()
```

To explain, you first import the libvirt module, then connect (conn) to the local QEMU hypervisor, adding its absolute address if it's a remote system. The "for" loop creates a domain object for each domain running on the node and, in sequence, suspends, resumes, and then destroys it, printing state information at every step. This, obviously, isn't something you'll necessarily want to run on a production deployment, but it illustrates the basic workings of the libvirt API.

Besides the hypervisor connection and domain sections, the libvirt API also provides access through network (virNetworkPtr), storage volume (virStorageVolPtr), and storage pool (virStoragePoolPtr) objects. You can also register with the API for automated notification of cluster life cycle events like domains booting, stopping, or resuming.

For more details, see the libvirt API documentation page: libvirt.org/html/index.html.

libvirt File Locations

As we've seen (with some exceptions), you'll find the automatically generated XML files that define your guests' properties in the **/etc/libvirt/qemu/** directory. The guest-specific source files that are similarly generated by **virt-install** (which, as we've also see, should only be edited using the *-edit tools provided for them) are kept in **/var/lib/libvirt/images/**.

As you can see from the file list just below, the /etc/libvirt/ directory contains a storage/ subirectory for pool XML files, and the qemu/ directory which includes the main domain *.XML configuration files, along with the networks/ directory for network configuration XML files.

```
$ pwd
/etc/libvirt
$
$ ls
libvirt.conf    lxc.conf    qemu        qemu-lockd.conf  virtlockd.conf
libvirtd.conf   nwfilter    qemu.conf   storage
$ cd qemu/networks
$ ls
autostart   default.xml
$
```

Resources:	
Project Home:	libvirt.org
Documentation:	libvirt.org/docs.html

vmbuilder

For a highly automated guest creation process, vmbuilder - or its Ubuntu-affiliated ubuntu-vm-builder wrapper - definitely has its charms.

```
# apt install ubuntu-vm-builder
```

On the surface, the command syntax may look a lot like virt-install, but there are two big differences. Rather than pointing the script to an OS image somewhere on the host, you just specify the distro you're after (Ubuntu, in this case) and the release version (Trusty), and vmbuilder will download it for you. But perhaps the bigger difference is the fact that there won't be any .XML file saved to your file system: the --libvirt argument tells libvirt to manage the configuration directly.

```
vmbuilder kvm ubuntu \
    --name new-ubuntu-vm
    --suite trusty \
    --flavour virtual \
    --addpkg=linux-image-generic \
    --addpkg=unattended-upgrades \
    --addpkg openssh-server \
    --addpkg=acpid \
    --arch amd64 \
    --libvirt qemu:///system \
    --user ubuntu \
    --name mypassword \
    --hostname=test \
    --pass default
```

Note: you will not be able to use virsh commands to manage your guests generated using vmbuilder unless you include the --libvirt qemu:///system argument. You can use either of:

```
# virsh -c qemu:///system
# virsh start new-ubuntu-vm
```

...to start your guest.

If you're building a more complex guest profile, you might like to load your arguments from a config file rather than including the whole, long string on the command line. This can be done with a vmbuilder.cfg file. By default, vmbuilder will look for either /etc/vmbuilder.cfg or ~/.vmbuilder.cfg, but you can write your own and call it from the command line.

```
# vmbuilder kvm ubuntu -c my-guest-file.cfg
```

Here's an example of a simple cgf file:

```
[DEFAULT]
arch = i386
ip = 10.0.4.100
part = vmbuilder.partition
user = ubuntu
name = ubuntu
pass = default
tmpfs = -
firstboot = boot.sh
firstlogin = login.sh

[ubuntu]
mirror = http://ca.archive.ubuntu.com/ubuntu/
suite = trusty
flavour = virtual
addpkg = openssh-server, apache2, apache2-utils, apache2.2-
common,libapache2-mod-php5, php5-cli, php5-gd, php5-ldap, php5-
mysql, mysql-server, unattended-upgrades, acpid

[kvm]
libvirt = qemu:///system
```

Command Cheat Sheet

Generate domain XML definition	virt-install -n my_vm -r 256 --vcpus=2
Domain XML file location	/etc/libvirt/qemu/
Help file	virsh help
Export XML file contents	virsh dumpxml my_vm > new_vm.xml
Create new domain	virsh create new_vm.xml
Define new object parameters	virsh vol-create-as new_image_lvm volume1 2G
List domains	virsh list
List resources	virsh *-list
Start a domain	virsh start my_vm
Shutdown a domain	virsh shutdown my_vm
Suspend a domain	virsh suspend my_vm
Restart suspended domain	virsh resume my_vm
Destroy domain	virsh destroy my_vm
Safely edit domain XML file	virsh edit my_vm
Safely edit network settings	virsh net-edit default
Safely edit storage pool settings	virsh pool-edit home
Safely edit network interface	virsh iface-edit lo
Create a copy of a pool	virsh vol-dumpxml --pool home > newvol.xml
Connect to domain as root	virsh -c qemu:///system
Connect to domain as non-root	virsh -c qemu:///session
Load disk into domain	virsh pool-define ~/shared_files_disk.xml
Mount a storage pool	virsh pool-start
Add disk to VM	virsh attach-device my_vm /etc/libvirt/storage/newdisk.xml

Test Yourself

1. Which directory contains the key libvirt configuration files?

a) /etc/default/libvirt

b) /var/lib/libvirt

c) /etc/libvirt/libvirt.d

d) /etc/libvirt

2. How do you launch an existing domain using libvirt from the command line?

a) virsh create filename.xml

b) virsh launch filename.xml

c) libvirt create filename.xml

d) libvirt launch filename.xml

3. When creating a new domain definition using virt-install from the command line, which flag points to a source iso file?

a) --disk

b) -n

c) -c

d) -r

4. Which of these is the best way to edit a libvirt XML file?

a) virsh edit my_vm

b) nano my_vm

c) virt-install my_vm

d) vi my_vm

5. In which of these locations are you most likely to find XML guest configuration files generated by virt-install?

a) /dev/kvm

b) /var/lib/libvirt/images

c) ~/.virtinst

d) /etc/libvirt/qemu

6. Which of these is NOT a value KVM/libvirt pool type?

a) netfs

b) DIR

c) virtimages

d) iSCSI

7. Which of these tags from a KVM .XML file would you use to set up incoming network access for a guest?

a) <target>

b) <pool>

c) <network>

d) <source>

Answer Key: 1:d,2:a,3:c,4:a,5:d,6:c,7:d

6. Cloud Management Tools

LPIC-304 Exam Objective 330.6

CloudStack

OpenStack

Eucalyptus

OpenNebula

In previous chapters we've seen how hypervisors (like Xen and KVM) and other virtualization technologies (including LXC, VirtualBox, and Docker) can be used to provision and administrate complex deployments involving multiple VMs. Technically, there is enough functionality built into each of those tools to successfully manage whatever infrastructure they serve, but that doesn't mean that there aren't sometimes better alternatives.

You will probably be especially interested in finding a third-party cloud management tool if your project can benefit from the many advantages of cloud computing – especially considering how complicated it can be to orchestrate the hundreds of moving parts that a large cloud environment can have. Just imagine how much fun you'll have directly managing unpredictable combinations of physical and virtual resources based both in local data centers and in public clouds!

So in this chapter, we'll describe four of the more widely adopted solutions: CloudStack, OpenStack, Eucalyptus, and OpenNebula. But before we get there, it might be worthwhile to make sure we're familiar with the way some terms are commonly used within the cloud world.

Cloud Terminology

Instance: The virtualized equivalent of a single computer server. Someone who "launches a cloud instance," will be given access and compute function pretty much exactly comparable to what he would have from a physical computer (or virtual machine).

Image: A template of a full software stack - including the base operating system - that can be automatically loaded on to a virtual instance as it's launched. On Amazon's AWS, for example, pre-built *Amazon Machine Images* (AMIs) can be shared and reused without limit.

Block storage: Blocks are segments of a physical storage device that can be abstracted and indexed by a file system, allowing data to be organized using any one of a number of systems. In the cloud world, block storage can be provided in the form of virtualized hard drives.

Object storage: Services (like AWS's S3) provide platforms to which individual files (or objects) can be saved along with their metadata and object ID.

Networks: Cloud environments will generally provide virtualized network tools that can simulate devices like NICs, routers, and firewalls. In some cases, as with AWS's Virtual Private Clouds (VPCs), entire multi-level network infrastructures are created, including subnets (Availability Zones), route tables, and distinct geographic regions.

SSH key injection: For virtualized instances, whose launch and shutdown life cycles can easily be automated, establishing secure connectivity with clients and administrators can be complex. SSH key injection scripts can be applied to automatically - and securely - insert usable public keys into new instances.

APIs: Application program interfaces (APIs) are protocols for programmatic access to application resources. Cloud platforms provide endpoint addresses that can be used by clients for accessing each one of your cloud resources. The APIs used by each cloud provider will have its own syntax and rules.

CloudStack

CloudStack is open source software governed by the Apache Software Foundation and supported by Cirtix Systems. CloudStack provides administration access through their browser UI, command line tools, and a RESTful API. Their toolkit includes user and account management and compute and networking orchestration, and can be configured for highly available and highly scalable deployments within security zones spread across multiple regions.

CloudStack supports all the major hypervisors: VMware, KVM, Citrix XenServer, Xen Cloud Platform (XCP), Oracle VM server and Microsoft Hyper-V.

What everyone wants to know - but is usually too afraid to ask - is what kind of integration a resource manager has with public cloud providers...and especially AWS. In CloudStack's case, the answer is that their API is compatible with Amazon's EC2 and S3.

CloudStack documentation is solid, but community support - while growing - can struggle to keep up with a quickly changing target.

OpenStack

OpenStack is also open source software managed under the Apache 2.0 license that can run with OVF, VMDK,VDI,VHD, and Raw machine image types. It also supports major hypervisor platforms including Xen and KVM and, to a lesser extent, VMware ESX, Citrix Xen server, and Microsoft's Hyper-V. Oracle VM is not supported.

OpenStack is built on modular components (Image server, Identity service, Dashboard, Networking, Block storage, Open storage, and AWS compatibility), which allows you to streamline your configuration by installing only those modules you actually need. Nevertheless, the initial configuration is, by reputation, complex and time consuming. Documentation and community support are both solid.

You manage resources through the OpenStack API, EC2 compatibility API, or the browser dashboard - which allows for self-service portals. Through the Orchestration tab on the dashboard, you can load templates that fully define the number and size of your VMs (which can be resized on the fly), and OS image they'll use. Config profiles are called "flavors".

OpenStack also has an "application-aware" metering service through which you can automate processes like customer billing and autoscaling.

Eucalyptus

By far the greatest strength of Eucalyptus - and probably the main reason that Hewlett-Packard purchased it back in 2014 - is its deep and formal integration with AWS services.

Eucalyptus allows you to apply AWS-like tools called (familiarly enough) Autoscaling, Elastic Load Balancing, and CloudWatch to your local clouds. You can even seamlessly share APIs, scripts, and machine images between the private and public parts of your deployments.

The product is available both in its free, open source version, and as the commercial Eucalyptus Enterprise Cloud.

OpenNebula

Finally, OpenNebula offers a high level of customization for resource isolation or multi-tiered deployments. It can interface with the full range of providers, including the Amazon EC2 Query API, OGF Open Cloud Computing Interface, and vCloud, and the Xen, KVM, and VMware hypervisors. The versatility enables all kinds of hardware/software and local/remote combinations but, to some degree, OpenNebula's "all-in-one" approach can lend itself nicely to smaller and simpler use cases.

Resources:
Project Home: opennebula.org
Documentation: opennebula.org/documentation

7. High Availability Concepts and Theory

LPIC-304 Exam Objective 334.1

Active/Active Cluster

Active/Passive Cluster

Availability

Session Handling

In this chapter, we will focus more on some of the larger architectural principles of cluster management than on any single technology solution. We will get to see some actual implementations a bit later, but for now, let's first make sure we're comfortable with the basics.

Running server operations using clusters of either physical or virtual computers is all about improving both reliability and performance over and above what you could expect from a single, high-powered server. You add reliability by avoiding hanging your entire infrastructure on a single point of failure (i.e., a single server). And you can increase performance through the ability to very quickly add computing power and capacity by scaling up and out.

This might happen through intelligently spreading your workloads among diverse geographic and demand environments (load balancing), providing backup servers that can be quickly brought into service in the event a working node fails (failover), optimizing the way your data tier is deployed, or allowing for fault tolerance through loosely coupled architectures.

We'll get to all that. First, though, here are some basic definitions:

Node: A single machine (either physical or virtual) running server operations independently on its own operating system. Since any single node can fail, meeting availability goals requires that multiple nodes operate as part of a cluster.

Cluster: Two or more server nodes running in coordination with each other to complete individual tasks as part of a larger service, where mutual awareness allows one or more nodes to compensate for the loss of another.

Server failure: The inability of a server node to respond adequately to client requests. This could be due to a complete crash, connectivity problems, or because it has been overwhelmed by high demand.

Failover: The way a cluster tries to accommodate the needs of clients orphaned by the failure of a single server node by launching or redirecting other nodes to fill a service gap. *Task reassignment*

Failback: The restoration of responsibilities to a server node as it recovers from a failure. *node recovery*

Replication: The creation of copies of critical data stores to permit reliable synchronous access from multiple server nodes or clients and to ensure they will survive disasters. Replication is also used to enable reliable load balancing.

Redundancy: The provisioning of multiple identical physical or virtual server nodes of which any one can adopt the orphaned clients of another one that fails.

Split brain: An error state in which network communication between nodes or shared storage has somehow broken down and multiple individual nodes, each believing it's the only node still active, continue to access and update a common data source. While this doesn't impact shared-nothing designs, it can lead to client errors and data corruption within shared clusters. *failed communication error state*

Fencing: To prevent split brain, the stonithd daemon can be configured to automatically shut down a malfunctioning node or to impose a virtual fence between it and the data resources of the rest of a cluster. As long as there is a chance that the node could still be active, but is not properly coordinating with the rest of the cluster, it will remain behind the fence. *Stonith* stands for "Shoot the other node in the head". Really. *Shutting down unresponsive nodes*

Quorum: You can configure fencing (or forced shutdown) to be imposed on nodes that have fallen out of contact with each other or with some shared resource. Quorum is often defined as more than half of all the nodes on the total cluster. Using such defined configurations, you avoid having two subclusters of nodes, each believing the other to be malfunctioning, attempting to knock the other one out. *numeric requirement for fencing*

Disaster Recovery: Your infrastructure can hardly be considered highly available if you've got no automated backup system in place along with an integrated and tested disaster recovery plan. Your plan will need to account for the redeployment of each of the servers in your custer.

Active/Passive Cluster

The idea behind service failover is that the sudden loss of any one node in a service cluster would quickly be made up by another node taking its place. For this to work, the IP address is automatically moved to the standby node in the event of a failover. Alternatively, network routing tools like load balancers can be used to redirect traffic away from failed nodes. The precise way failover happens depends on the way you have configured your nodes.

Only one node will initially be configured to serve clients, and will continue to do so alone until it somehow fails. The responsibility for existing and new clients will then shift (i.e., "failover") to the passive - or backup - node that until now has been kept passively in reserve. Applying the model to multiple servers or server room components (like power supplies), n+1 redundancy provides just enough resources for the current demand plus one more unit to cover for a failure.

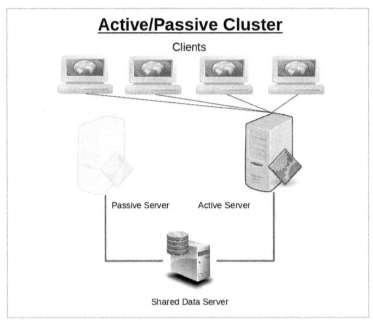

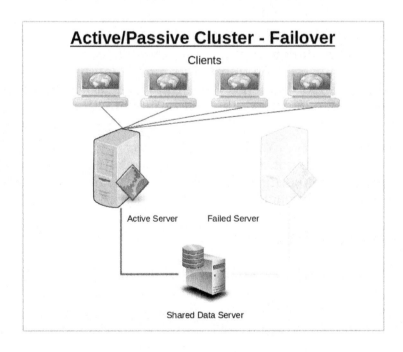

Active/Active Cluster

A cluster using an active/active design will have two or more identically configured nodes independently serving clients.

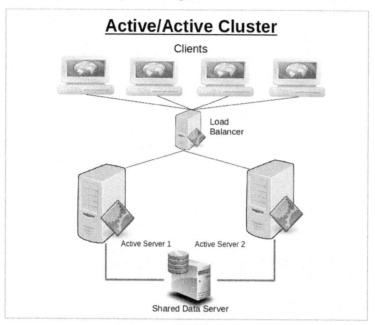

Should one node fail, its clients will automatically connect with the second node and, as far as resources permit, receive full resource access.

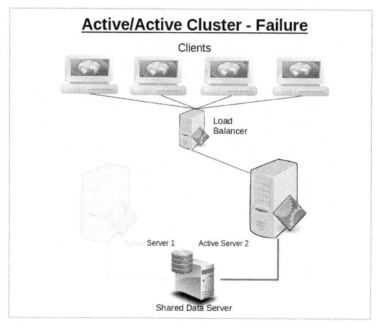

Once the first node recovers or is replaced, clients will once again be split between both server nodes.

The primary advantage of running active/active clusters lies in the ability to efficiently balance a workload between nodes and even networks. The load balancer - which directs all requests from clients to available servers - is configured to monitor node and network activity and use some predetermined algorithm to route traffic to those nodes best able to handle it. Routing policies might follow a round-robin pattern, where client requests are simply alternated between available nodes, or by a preset weight where one node is favored over another by some ratio.

Having a passive node acting as a stand-by replacement for its partner in an active/passive cluster configuration provides significant built-in redundancy. If your operation absolutely requires uninterrupted service and seamless failover transitions, then some variation of an active/passive architecture should be your goal.

Shared-Nothing vs. Shared-Disk Clusters

One of the guiding principles of distributed computing is to avoid having your operation rely on any single point of failure. That is, every resource should be either actively replicated (redundant) or independently replaceable (failover), and there should be no single element whose failure could bring down your whole service.

Now, imagine that you're running a few dozen nodes that all rely on a single database server for their function. Even though the failure of any number of the nodes will not affect the continued health of those nodes that remain, should the *database* go down, the entire cluster would become useless. Nodes in a shared-nothing cluster, however, will (usually) maintain their own databases so that - assuming they're being properly synced and configured for ongoing transaction safety - no external failure will impact them.

This will have a more significant impact on a load balanced cluster, as each load balanced node has a constant and critical need for simultaneous access to the data. The passive node on a simple failover system, however, might be able to survive some time without access.

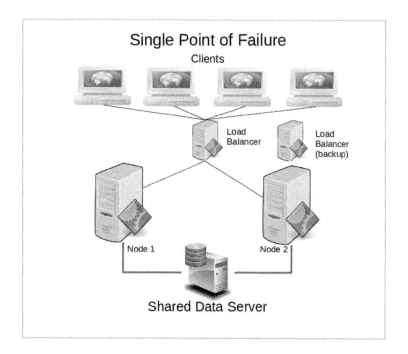

Shared nothing

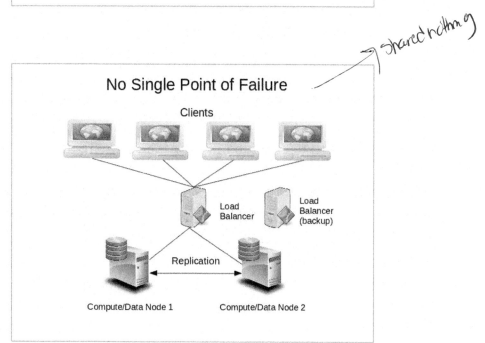

While such a setup might slow down the way the cluster responds to some requests - partly because fears of split-brain failures might require periodic fencing through stonith - the trade off can be justified for mission critical deployments where reliability is the primary consideration.

Availability

When designing your cluster, you'll need to have a pretty good sense of just how tolerant you can be of failure. Or, in other words, given the needs of the people or machines consuming your services, how long can a service disruption last before the mob comes pouring through your front gates with pitch forks and flaming torches. It's important to know this, because the amount of redundancy you build into your design will have an enormous impact on the down-times you will eventually face.

Obviously, the system you build for a service that can go down for a weekend without anyone noticing will be very different from an e-commerce site whose customers expect 24/7 access. At the very least, you should generally aim for an availability average of at least 99% - with some operations requiring significantly higher real-world results. 99% up time would translate to a loss of less than a total of four days out of every year.

There is a relatively simple formula you can use to build a useful estimate of Availability (A). The idea is to divide the Mean Time Before Failure by the Mean Time Before Failure plus Mean Time To Repair.

$$A = MTBF / (MTBF + MTTR)$$

The closer the value of A comes to 1, the more highly available your cluster will be. To obtain a realistic value for MTBF, you'll probably need to spend time exposing a real system to some serious punishment, and watching it carefully for software, hardware, and networking failures. I suppose you could also consult the published life cycle metrics of hardware vendors or large-scale consumers like Backblaze to get an idea of how long heavily-used hardware can be expected to last.

The MTTR will be a product of the time it takes your cluster to replace the functionality of a server node that's failed (a process that's similar to, though not identical with, disaster recovery - which focuses on quickly replacing failed hardware and connectivity). Ideally, that would be a value as close to zero seconds as possible.

Server Availability

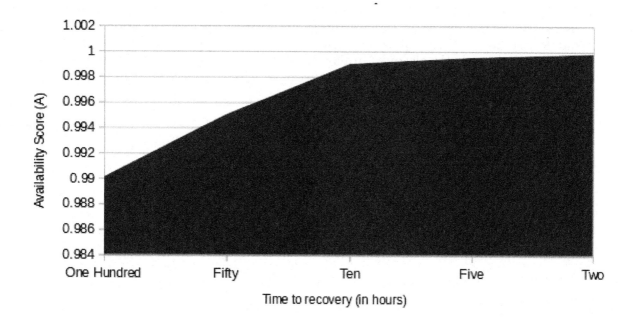

The problem is that, in the real world, there are usually far too many unknown variables for this formula to be truly accurate, as nodes running different software configurations and built with hardware of varying profiles and ages will have a wide range of life expectancies. Nevertheless, it can be a good tool to help you identify the cluster design that's best for your project.

With that information, you can easily generate an estimate of how much overall downtime your service will likely in the course of an entire year.

A related consideration, if you're deploying your resources on a third-party platform provider like VMWare or Amazon Web Services, is the provider's Service Level Agreement (SLA). Amazon's EC2, for instance, guarantees that their compute instances and block store storage devices will deliver a Monthly Uptime Percentage of at least 99.95% - which is less than five hours' down time per year. AWS will issue credits for months in which they missed their targets - though not nearly enough to compensate for the total business costs of your downtime. With that information, you can arrange for a level of service redundancy that's suitable for your unique needs.

Naturally, as a service provider to your own customers, you may need to publish your own SLA based on your MTBF and MTTR estimates.

Session Handling

For any server-client relationship, the data generated by stateful HTTP sessions needs to be saved in a way that makes it available for future interactions. Cluster architectures can introduce serious complexity into these relationships, as the specific server a client or user interacts with might change between one step and the next.

To illustrate, imagine you're logged onto Amazon.com, browsing through their books on LPIC training, and periodically adding an item to your cart (hopefully, more copies of this book). By the time you're ready to enter your payment information and check out, however, the server you used to browse may no longer even exist. How will your current server know which books you decided to purchase?

I don't know exactly how Amazon handles this, but the problem is often addressed through a data replication tool like memcached running on an external node (or nodes). The goal is to provide constant access to a reliable and consistent data source to any node that might need it.

Test Yourself

1. Which of these High Availability terms refers to a crashed server's recovery and return to service?

a) Failover

b) Failback

c) Quorum

d) Fencing

2. Which of the following HA modes allows for load balancing?

a) Active/Passive

b) Shared-All

c) Shared-Volume

d) Active/Active

3. Which of these will calculate your system's availability (A)?

a) $A = MTBF / (MTBF + MTTR)$

b) $A = MTBF * (MTTR - MTBF)$

c) $A = MTTR / (MTBF / MTTR)$

d) $E = MC^2$

4. How does a cluster manage session handling for clients?

a) Stateful HTTP sessions and data replication

b) Stateless HTTP sessions and data replication

c) RESTful services and data replication

d) Stateless HTTP sessions alone

Answer Key: 1:b,2:d,3:a,4:a

8. Load Balanced Clusters

LPIC-304 Exam Objective 334.2

LVS (Linux Virtual Server)

Keepalived

ldirectord

HAProxy

To ensure that some server resources are not overburdened by network traffic while others sit idle - or that traffic isn't sent to unresponsive nodes (or can be reassigned if it was) - a well-designed network will route client requests intelligently. In this chapter, we'll look at four approaches to the problem of applying network awareness to the way you route packets among node clusters.

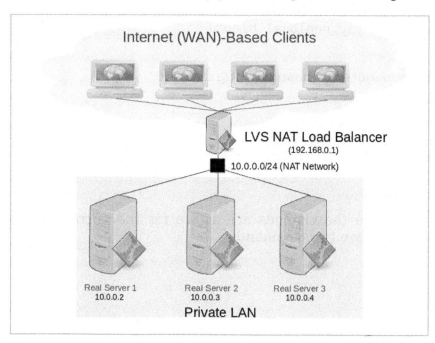

In every case, however, your load balancing server will sit between the Internet (or whichever network where your users/guests live) and the private network that hosts your nodes. All incoming traffic will move through your load balancing machine which will act as a kind of modified router.

Linux Virtual Server

LVS is load balancing software for systems using the Linux kernel. It's managed by IP load balancing software (IPVS) through the **ipvsadm** command line tool. While, as we will see, you can use larger packages like **Keepalived** and **ldirectord** to manage LVS, there is actually a great deal you can do with LVS directly from the command line.

Your first step (after brewing yourself a good, strong coffee and checking your email) should be to load the ip_vs kernel module and confirm it's there:

```
# modprobe ip_vs
# cat /proc/net/ip_vs
IP Virtual Server version 1.2.1 (size=4096)
Prot LocalAddress:Port Scheduler Flags
  -> RemoteAddress:Port Forward Weight ActiveConn InActConn
$
```

Install the **ipvsadm** package.

However you plan to execute load balancing, your LVS server will be routing requests between external clients and the cluster nodes you're serving. Therefore you'll need to enable packet forwarding through the **/etc/sysctl.conf** file (by default, this is normally disabled) and non-local IP address binding. Make sure these two lines exist (and are uncommented):

```
net.ipv4.ip_forward=1
net.ipv4.ip_nonlocal_bind=1
```

Then propagate the change using sysctl.

```
# sysctl -p
net.ipv4.ip_forward = 1
net.ipv4.ip_nonlocal_bind = 1
#
```

To make sure the changes are active for the current session on CentOS, you would run these two commands:

```
# /sbin/sysctl -w net.ipv4.ip_forward=1
# /sbin/sysctl -w net.ipv4.ip_nonlocal_bind=1
```

On Ubuntu, this is how your **/etc/default/ipvsadm** file will look by default, but you may (or may not) need to edit it to get the service started. We'll discuss the daemons later.

```
# ipvsadm
# if you want to start ipvsadm on boot set this to true
AUTO="false"
# daemon method (none|master|backup)
DAEMON="none"
# use interface (eth0,eth1...)
IFACE="eth0"
# syncid to use
SYNCID="1"
```

The equivalent file on CentOS will be /etc/sysconfig/ipvsadm-config.

You can query the status of LVS using:

```
# ipvsadm -L -n
IP Virtual Server version 1.2.1 (size=4096)
Prot LocalAddress:Port Scheduler Flags
-> RemoteAddress:Port Forward Weight ActiveConn InActConn
#
```

Start the service using systemctl:

```
# systemctl start ipvsadm
```

Next, you need to clear any existing tables (**-C**), add (**-A**) a virtual network service (**192.168.0.100:80**), and references (**-r**) to your real servers (**10.0.0.2:80**, **10.0.0.3:80** and **10.0.0.4:80**):

```
# ipvsadm -C
# ipvsadm -A -t 192.168.0.100:80 -s wlc
# ipvsadm -a -t 192.168.0.100:80 -r 10.0.0.2:80 -m
# ipvsadm -a -t 192.168.0.100:80 -r 10.0.0.3:80 -m
# ipvsadm -a -t 192.168.0.100:80 -r 10.0.0.4:80 -m
```

Now confirm that your configuration is the way you want it.

```
# ipvsadm -l
IP Virtual Server version 1.2.1 (size=4096)
Prot LocalAddress:Port Scheduler Flags
  -> RemoteAddress:Port Forward Weight ActiveConn InActConn
#
```

You can save a configuration using **ipvsadm-save** (or **/etc/rc.d/init.d/ipvsadm save**, depending on your system) and restore it with **ipvsadm-restore**.

LVS Forwarding

LVS can be designed to forward traffic in any one of three ways: NAT (LVS-NAT), Direct Routing (LVS-DR), and Tunneling (LVS-Tun) , each with its own strengths and weaknesses.

For NAT forwarding, a load balancer would receive, read, and rewrite the destination IP address and, optionally, port number of the IP header for all inbound client requests: forwarding requests to individual application server nodes within any private NAT network. To ensure that it reaches the correct client, the node's response - including all the data packets being provided to the client - would then be sent back to the client through the same balancer via the default gateway.

NAT forwarding (which can be invoked using ipvsadm with -m) has the advantage of being relatively simple to set up and will work smoothly with nodes running any operating system that supports TCP/IP (i.e., any operating system released over the past few centuries). The down side is that the number of requests a single NAT server can handle will be limited by its own resources and the bandwidth available to access both internal and external networks.

Direct Routing (which takes the -g flag) and Tunneling (-i) are clever workarounds to this problem that work, but can require significant configuration. LVS routers (balancers) using Direct Routing send client requests to real servers (identifying them by MAC address), which then route responses directly to the clients, rather than back the way they arrived. The balancer, therefore, only has to handle the much smaller *incoming* packets, allowing it to manage traffic for many more servers.

Tunneling requires a preexisting *IP in IP* tunnel between the LVS balancer and the real server (node). When the balancer receives a client request, it forwards the data through the tunnel addressed to the appropriate real server node, which will respond to the client directly, again bypassing the balancer bottleneck altogether.

One complication of DR and Tunnel forwarding is known as the ARP (Address Resolution Protocol) problem, where both the LVS balancer and a real server can become identified by the network with a single IP address. You should be aware of the problem and of various methods for resolving it, including placing your local targets within networks separated from the LVS server's virtual IP address, supplying the VIP's actual MAC address to the client, and forwarding packets based on your realservers' MAC address.

The ipvsadm package includes a master connection synchronization daemon (for the master load balancer within a cluster) and a backup connection synchronization daemon that should be running on a backup balancer. If the backup balancer is ever to successfully take over should the master fail, it will need full awareness of the current states of all client sessions. Synchronization (replication) is the job of this deamon.

This process can also be managed through Pacemaker.

Now let's go back and take another look at these earlier real server configuration examples:

```
# ipvsadm -A -t 192.168.0.100:80 -s wlc
# ipvsadm -a -t 192.168.0.100:80 -r 10.0.0.2:80 -m
# ipvsadm -a -t 192.168.0.100:80 -r 10.0.0.3:80 -m
# ipvsadm -a -t 192.168.0.100:80 -r 10.0.0.4:80 -m
```

-m sets the packet forwarding method to masquerading (NAT). A tunneling connection would require **-i**, and **-g** signifies gateway routing. When the **-p** flag is used, these protocols will produce **sticky sessions** where client-server relationships remain persistent.

wlc stands for "Weighted Least-Connection" which is a scheduling algorithm that prefers routing jobs to those servers with the fewest existing connections. You could edit the algorithm used for a particular service using **-E**. Changing this example to **wrr** - Weighted Round Robin - would tell the load balancer to send jobs to real servers in proportion to their assigned weight.

```
# ipvsadm -E -t 192.168.0.100:80 -s wrr
```

You can assign weights to real servers using the **-w** flag.

Besides wlc, other available algorithms include:

Destination Hashing Scheduling (-dh): This bases server assignments on hashes created from *destination* IP addresses.

Source Hashing Scheduling (-sh): This bases server assignments on hashes created from *source* IP addresses.

Never Queue Scheduling (-nq) : When an idle server is available, it will be used. When all servers are currently busy, a job will be sent to the one likely to complete it first.

ldirectord

ldirectord is a daemon that can monitor and manage the accessibility of the real or virtual servers provided by the Linux Virtual Server (LVS). You can install ldirectord directly from the repositories (although it seems to have been removed from the RHEL 6 default repository and replaced with Piranha).

Basic file system information is controlled through the ldirectord Perl script in **/etc/init.d/**, which includes the path to the ldirectord daemon and configuration file:

```
$ less /etc/init.d/ldirectord
NAME=ldirectord
DAEMON="/usr/sbin/$NAME"
CONFIG="/etc/default/$NAME"
$
```

The **/etc/default/ldirectord** file does little more than point to the default ldirectord configuration file, which is **/etc/ldirectord.cf** in this case:

```
$ less /etc/default/ldirectord
CONFIG_FILE=/etc/ldirectord.cf
$
```

The **ldirectord.cf** file defines the client-facing virtual IP address (192.168.0.105, in this example), and the addresses of the real servers (there are three in this example). The load balancing algorithm used here is **Weighted Round Robin** (wrr). Besides Weighted Round Robin, available algorithms include Round-Robin Scheduling, Least-Connection, Weighted Least-Connections, and Destination Hash Scheduling.

```
$ less /etc/ldirectord.cf
checktimeout=3
checkinterval=5
autoreload=yes
logfile="/var/log/ldirectord.log"
quiescent=no
virtual=192.168.0.105:80
        real=10.0.0.2:80 gate
        real=10.0.0.3:80 gate
        real=10.0.0.4:80 gate
        scheduler=wrr
        protocol=tcp
        checktype=connect
        checkport=80
$
```

The value of **checktimeout** determines how long (in seconds) ldirectord will retry health checks before declaring the server dead. **checkinterval** sets the interval between checks. **autoreload** tells ldirectord to continuously check the configuration file for changes. **quiescent**, when it set to "yes", allows realservers to be taken offline gracefully, allowing current sessions to continue, but blocking new sessions. The value "no" will remove a server from the kernel's LVS table when it goes down. Finally, **checktype** controls what kind of checks will be performed, including connect, external, negotiate, off, on, and ping.

You're ready to start up your ldirectord service.

```
# Systemctl start ldirectord
```

Use ipvsadm to confirm that your configuration is live.

```
# ipvsadm -L -n
```

Now access and refresh the virtual IP address from your browser and you should see your real servers' contents displayed according to your scheduler algorithm.

Resources:	
Project Home:	linuxvirtualserver.org
Documenation:	linuxvirtualserver.org/Documents.html

Keepalived

When building your infrastructure, a primary design consideration is, wherever possible, avoiding single points of failure. Since all hardware - and most software - will eventually fail, you should never rely on any single device for a critical service. To this end, redundancy is your friend. The role that load balancing plays in all this is to ensure that incoming traffic is routed as efficiently as possible to the best server resources available.

Keepalived can manage redundancy by performing health checks and implementing a Hot Standby protocol on top of an LVS framework, its virtual IPs (VIPs), and real server pools. But, since even routers can (and will) fail, Keepalived will also integrate the Virtual Router Redundancy Protocol (VRRP) for director failover management.

The ultimate goal of it all is to provide clients with a single (virtual) IP address that connects them to whichever server node is best suited for the task. One way that Keepalived does this is by regularly checking the health of your backend servers. Keepalived uses the genhash tool to generate MD5 hashes from server-based web pages using either HTTP or (through the **-use-ssl** argument) HTTPS. These hashes are used verify the operational status of backend servers.

Let's illustrate all this with a simple, two-node Keepalived deployment. We'll start by installing Keepalived and the Apache webserver package on two Ubuntu 16.04 servers (although you might normally prefer to keep your webservers on separate machines from a load balancer). As older repositories might contain outdated and/or buggy versions, we may want to compile our own copy of Keepalived. (The repository package for both apt-get and Yum systems is called **keepalived**.) We will do this on both of our nodes.

I'm sure you already know the drill:

```
# apt install build-essential libssl-dev
$ wget http://www.keepalived.org/software/keepalived-1.2.19.tar.gz
$ tar xzvf keepalived-1.2.19.tar.gz
$ cd keepalived
# ./configure
# make
# make install
```

Use the usual systemd tools to control Keepalived behavior. Now, we'll create a keepalived directory in **/etc/**.

```
# mkdir -p /etc/keepalived
```

...along with a configuration file:

```
# nano /etc/keepalived/keepalived.conf
```

What follows is a sample **keepalived.conf** file.

```
! Configuration File for keepalived

vrrp_instance VI_1 {
    state MASTER
    interface eth0
    virtual_router_id 51
    priority 100
    advert_int 1
    authentication {
        auth_type AH
        auth_pass topsecret
    }
    virtual_ipaddress {
        192.168.200.16
        192.168.200.17
        192.168.200.18
    }
}

virtual_server 192.168.200.16 443 {
    delay_loop 6
    lb_algo rr
    lb_kind NAT
    persistence_timeout 50
    protocol TCP

    real_server 192.168.201.100 80 {
        weight 1
      HTTP_GET {
            url {
              path / testurl/test.jsp
              digest ec90a42b99ea9a2f5ecbe213ac9eba03
            }
            url {
              path /testurl2/test.jsp
              digest 640205b7b0fc66c1ea91c463fac6334c
            }
            connect_timeout 3
            nb_get_retry 3
            delay_before_retry 3
        }
    }
}

virtual_server 192.168.200.17 80 {
    delay_loop 6
    lb_algo rr
    lb_kind NAT
    persistence_timeout 50
    protocol TCP

    real_server 192.168.201.100 80 {
```

```
                    weight 1
                    HTTP_GET {
                        url {
                          path /testurl/test.jsp
                          digest 640205b7b0fc66c1ea91c463fac6334c
                        }
                        connect_timeout 3
                        nb_get_retry 3
                        delay_before_retry 3
                    }
                }
            }
```

Notice the three addresses assigned as virtual IPs. These will be the target addresses for all incoming traffic. The file also defines a virtual server and a real server along with their connection and configuration profiles. The **sorry_server** line tells Keepalived where to send traffic should everything else fail. The name comes from the server's function: "We are sorry, but this resource is not available at the present time..."

You will create a similar **keepalived.conf** file on your **secondary node** with the same value for **virtual_ipaddress**, but a number lower than 150 for **priority**.

So we can illustrate that the failover is working, create a simple index.html file in the html root of each server identifying the server. Here's what I used for the primary server:

```
echo "Hi. Welcome to the primary server." > sudo /var/www/html/
index.html
```

...And on the secondary server:

```
echo "Hi. Welcome to the secondary server." > sudo /var/www/html/
index.html
```

Start up Keepalived (on both servers):

```
# systemctl start keepalived
```

In a browser, visit your virtual IP address (192.168.200.16, in our example). The primary server page should appear. Then simulate a failure by shutting down Keepalived on the primary server.

```
# systemctl stop keepalived
```

...And reload your browser. You should now have failed over to the secondary browser.

HAProxy

Within the context of the OSI Networking Model, LVS does its work at Layer Four (or Layer Three, in the case of LVS-DR - Direct Routing). This makes it ideal for balancing based on connections controlled by simple health checks. LVS is also very fast at what it does. However, if you require balancing algorithms that filter for HTTP response time or that can redirect traffic based on header parameters, then a Layer Seven balancer like HAProxy might work better.

Installation and Configuration

All the magic happens in the haproxy.cfg file that's kept in the **/etc/haproxy/** directory. But first we'll see about installing the **HAProxy** package and getting it running.

When we're ready, we'll need to make a simple edit to the HAProxy file in the **/etc/default/** directory, so that the value of ENABLED is 1

```
ENABLED=1
```

Again, once we're ready, we start up haproxy, get it going with systemctl:

```
# systemctl enable haproxy
# systemctl start haproxy
```

One important note: the server (or container) you choose to use for HAProxy should be dedicated to just this function. Any other services you run - especially services like Apache that use port 80 - will get in the way. That said, there are some infrastructure tasks that can be handed off to HAProxy, like SSL offloading, where you HAProxy server takes on header encryption responsibilities for packets rather than relying on sometimes overworked application servers.

With all that administrative stuff out of the way, we can turn our attention to the haproxy.cfg file. Here's what it might look like by default:

```
global
    log /dev/log local0
    log /dev/log local1 notice
    chroot        /var/lib/haproxy
    stats socket       /run/haproxy/admin.sock mode 660 level admin
    stats timeout        30s
    user          haproxy
    group         haproxy
    daemon

    # Default SSL material locations
    ca-base      /etc/ssl/certs
    crt-base     /etc/ssl/private

    # Default ciphers to use on SSL-enabled listening sockets.
    # For more information, see ciphers(1SSL).
      ssl-default-bind-ciphers kEECDH+aRSA+AES:kRSA+AES:+AES256:RC4-
SHA:!kEDH:!LOW:!EXP:!MD5:!aNULL:!eNULL

defaults
    log               global what is
    mode              http
    option            httplog
    option            dontlognull
    timeout connect   5000
    timeout client    50000
    timeout server    50000
    errorfile 400     /etc/haproxy/errors/400.http
    errorfile 403     /etc/haproxy/errors/403.http
    errorfile 408     /etc/haproxy/errors/408.http
    errorfile 500     /etc/haproxy/errors/500.http
    errorfile 502     /etc/haproxy/errors/502.http
    errorfile 503     /etc/haproxy/errors/503.http
    errorfile 504     /etc/haproxy/errors/504.http
```

The **global** section sets the environment parameters for HAProxy - including its user and group, log behavior, SSL ciphers, and the way that HAProxy will be relatively isolated from the rest of the system within chroot.

The **defaults** section controls timeout options and the messages that will be displayed in response to error events. All of these values can be changed to fit your specific needs.

To enable actual load balancing, we might now add two more sections to the config file that look something like this:

```
frontend mylistener
    bind *:80
    mode http
    default_backend nodes

backend nodes
    mode http
    balance roundrobin
    option forwardfor
    http-request set-header X-Forwarded-Port %[dst_port]
    http-request add-header X-Forwarded-Proto https if { ssl_fc }
    option httpchk HEAD / HTTP/1.1\r\nHost:localhost
    server server01 10.0.0.3:80 check
    server server02 10.0.0.4:80 check
    server server03 10.0.0.5:80 check
```

Activate Health checks

The **frontend** section (which I called "mylistener") tells HAProxy to listen for all incoming HTTP traffic coming through port 80 via *any* interface (as directed by the "*"), and to then distribute it among the servers defined by backend nodes. You can also set **mode** to the TCP protocol.

The **backend** section sets the balancing algorithm as round robin, meaning that traffic will be forwarded to each server following a regular cycle. **option forwardfor** allows clients to see the application server's IP address, rather than that of the load balancer. The two **http-request** lines include header information to tell our application servers enough about the requests (i.e., their port and scheme) to know how to properly respond. The **option httpchk** line activates HAProxy's health checks of our servers. Finally, the three **server** lines point HAProxy to our three application servers and, through "check", telling it that all three should receive health checks.

If, say, one of our servers has a higher hardware capacity and we'd like it to receive more than its share of traffic, we could assign higher or lower weights to nodes in the pool by adding relative weight values to each server line, something like this:

```
server server01 10.0.0.3:80 check weight 20
server server02 10.0.0.4:80 check weight 10
server server03 10.0.0.5:80 check weight 5
```

In any case, should a health check against a particular server fail, incoming traffic will be redirected towards the other servers regardless of the normal algorithm's preferences.

If you want to enforce "sticky sessions" so that sessions will (when possible) always use the same server, you would add a **cookie** entry to the backend section that might look like this:

```
cookie COOKIE_NAME prefix
```

You would then add the "cookie" directive to each server line, like this:

```
server server01 10.0.0.3:80 cookie check
server server02 10.0.0.4:80 cookie check
server server03 10.0.0.5:80 cookie check
```

Besides round robin (and variations of those algorithms I mentioned above in relation to LVS), there are other balancing algorithms you can apply, including:

balance leastconn: This favors servers with the lowest number of current connections. leastconn is particularly useful for sessions requiring shorter connections, like HTTP.

balance source: Using this algorithm bases server choice on a hash of the source IP address, which is divided by the total weight of running servers. This is an attempt to maintain session connectivity wherever possible for clients that can't accept cookies.

uri: This algorithm bases server choice on a hash of the left part of URI (i.e., before the question mark) which is divided by the total weight of the running servers. You can control the number of characters to be considered with the **len** parameter, and the number of directory levels to include with **depth**. This is used to maintain session URI/server connectivity.

url_param: Here, service choice is based on a hash of the param value, divided by running server weight.

Access Control Lists (ACLs)

You can also control HAProxy traffic from within the haproxy.cfg file through ACLs. You add ACL lines to the frontend section of the file like this:

```
acl is_domain_1 url_beg -i domain1.com
acl is_domain_2 url_beg -i domain2.com
```

In this example, "**is_domain_n**" is the name I gave this rule, "**url_beg**" requires that the requesting URL should *start* with domain1.com, and **-i** tells HAProxy to ignore case (i.e., upper or lower case). Besides url_beg, other matching options include path_beg, path_end, path_sub, path_reg, url_end, url_sub, and url_reg.

You'll need to tell HAProxy what to do with a request that meets an ACL condition using a use_backend line that points to a backend section.

```
use_backend domain1.com if is_domain_1
use_backend domain2.com if is_domain_2
default_backend domain0.com
```

HAProxy includes a number of pre-defined ACL rules like FALSE, which prevents any match of a condition, and TRUE, which tells HAProxy to consider all packets as matching. You can use rules like this to fully open or close access to a server.

Note: you can include multiple backend sections in a config file, each representing individual servers or even clusters of servers. If a request doesn't match the conditions of any ACL rule, then it will be directed to the default backend.

Command Cheat Sheet

Load ip_vs kernel module	modprobe ip_vs
Uncomment in /etc/sysctl.conf	net.ipv4.ip_forward=1
	net.ipv4.ip_nonlocal_bind=1
Propogate change	sysctl -p
Query LVS status	ipvsadm -L -n
Launch ipvsadm on CentOS	chkconfig ipvsadm on
Clear existing tables	ipvsadm -C
Add a virtual network	ipvsadm -A -t 192.168.0.100:80 -s wlc
Add reference to real server	ipvsadm -a -t 192.168.0.100:80 -r 10.0.0.30:80
Save configuration	ipvsadm -S
Assign routing algorithm	ipvsadm -E -t 192.168.0.100:80 -s wrr

Resources:	
Project Home:	haproxy.org
Documenation:	haproxy.org/#docs

Test Yourself

1. Which of the following operates at level seven of the OSI Networking Model (ignoring their health check functionality)?

a) LVS

b) HAProxy

c) ldirectord

d) Keepalived

2. Which file do you use to configure packet forwarding?

a) /etc/ipvs.adm

b) /etc/default/ipvsadm

c) /var/lib/ipvs/ipvsadm

d) /etc/sysctl.conf

3. Which of the following will tell a backup load balancer to monitor for multicasts from the master?

a) ipvsadm --start-deamon master

b) ipvsadm --start-deamon listen

c) ipvsadm --start-deamon backup

d) ipvsadm -L -n

4. Which of the following Keepalived tools does NOT relate directly to node management?

a) Hot Standby

b) VRRP

c) Health checks

d) genhash

5. Which one of the following sections of the haproxy.cfg file controls the balance algorithm HAProxy will use?

a) frontend

b) defaults

c) global

d) backend

Answer Key: 1:b,2:d,3:c,4:b,5:d

9. Failover Clusters

LPIC-304 Exam Objective 334.3

Pacemaker

Installation

Cluster Failover Management - crm

Enterprise Resources

Pacemaker - Introduction

Unlike the load balancing tools we saw in the last chapter whose primary approach to high availability was through intelligent routing, a failover cluster, while often having deeply complex relationships with backend dependencies, introduces a level of redundancy to provide near-instant replacements for any cluster nodes that might fail.

Using clustered servers to optimize application failover has obvious benefits, but it can also get really complicated, really quickly. Remember: the nodes of a cluster aren't controlled by a server host somewhere, but act independently of each other as peers.

The current state of that art is the ClusterLabs Pacemaker project, which is normally deployed along with a software stack that includes Corosync. Pacemaker's job is managing services and ensuring that multiple independent cluster nodes aren't unnecessarily duplicating - and potentially corrupting - services. Pacemaker uses Corosync (which was derived from the OpenAIS project) to coordinate and communicate between the Pacemaker daemons running on each separate node. (You should also be aware of Heartbeat which - while sharing common origins - is a cluster resource manager/messaging and membership layer alternative to Pacemaker and Corosync.)

With cluster technologies and the specific software stacks used for deployments changing as quickly is they do, you will need to be particulary careful to closely monitor developments within the industry.

Functional Design

Communication between nodes - which includes controlling cluster membership - is managed by **Consensus Cluster Membership** (CCM).

Since keeping the nodes as aware of each other as possible is so important for healthy clusters, reliably moving and managing data across the network is critical. The **Cluster Information Base** (CIB) remains aware of the status of all configurations and resources, along with the way they're working with each other. The information CIB keeps is automatically synchronized through immediate updates to all the nodes of a cluster. This information is used by the **Policy Engine** (PEngine) to calculate how the cluster should change to adapt to any new developments.

CIB XML data is kept in the /var/lib/pacemaker/cib/cib.xml file (which, as we'll see a bit later, should never be edited directly). Here's an example of a simple cib.xml file:

```
<cib        crm_feature_set="3.0.10"        validate-with="pacemaker-2.3"
epoch="7" num_updates="0" admin_epoch="0" cib-last-written="Wed Feb
24    04:50:14    2016"    update-origin="pacemaker1"    update-
client="cibadmin" update-user="root" have-quorum="0" dc-uuid="1">
  <configuration>
    <crm_config>
      <cluster_property_set id="cib-bootstrap-options">
        <nvpair id="cib-bootstrap-options-have-watchdog" name="have-
            watchdog" value="false"/>
        <nvpair id="cib-bootstrap-options-dc-version" name="dc-
            version" value="1.1.13-10.el7_2.2-44eb2dd"/>
        <nvpair id="cib-bootstrap-options-cluster-infrastructure"
            name="cluster-infrastructure" value="corosync"/>
        <nvpair id="cib-bootstrap-options-cluster-name" name=
            "cluster-name" value="mycluster"/>
        <nvpair id="cib-bootstrap-options-stonith-enabled"
            name="stonith-enabled" value="false"/>
        <nvpair id="cib-bootstrap-options-no-quorum-policy"
            name="no-quorum-policy" value="ignore"/>
      </cluster_property_set>
    </crm_config>
    <nodes>
      <node id="1" uname="MyNode1"/>
      <node id="2" uname="MyNode2"/>
    </nodes>
    <resources/>
    <constraints/>
  </configuration>
</cib>
```

The PEngine will send the resulting instructions to the **Designated Coordinator** (DC).

"Designated? Designated by whom?" you ask. Pacemaker has a built-in algorithm that selects - and, if necessary, replaces - the CRMd running on one of the cluster nodes to control this part of the process. CRMd, by the way, stands for **Cluster Resource Management daemon**, which will be given infrastructure management cluster tasks by the DC. The DC could also execute tasks directly through the LRMd (**Local Resource Management Daemon**), whose job it is to interact with resource agent scripts.

Resource Agents

A "resource agent" of one or another class, is code or a script that acts as an interface between a cluster resource (like an Apache web service running on a node) and Pacemaker, stopping and starting a resource, or reporting on it's status and health. When Pacemaker gets a report of a failure, it might restart the service but, in that fails, can begin fencing off and replacing the offending node.

Assuming they're actually compliant, the OCF (Open Cluster Framework) class can monitory operations and interpret init scripts (as part of the Linux Standard Base, or LSB) in the /etc/init.d directory of any local machine within a cluster. OCF is the most common class for controlling cluster resources and I'll provide an example a bit later in this chapter.

Pacemaker can also make use of any "unit files" that might be present on individual machines running systemd, or "jobs" on Upstart machines (like Ubuntu before version 15.04). If there are files of multiple system services types within a single cluster, Pacemaker will look for named services on a local machine first from a LSB init script, then from a systemd unit file, and finally from an Upstart job.

Pacemaker can also interface with Nagios plugins to monitor resources on remote containers.

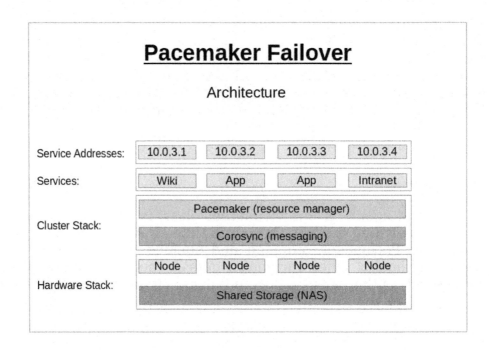

The Stonith class is for fencing off nodes. Stonith, by the way, stands for "Shoot The Other Node In The Head" - as that's pretty much what a cluster manager will do if it detects that a node has gone rogue. A stonith device is a resource that the stonithd daemon is able to manage. Stonith can actually be set to manage physical devices like Lights-Out modules and UPS power supplies, meaning that events could prompt the daemon to simply shut down a physical server if necessary.

Installation

Installing and deploying the stack across your cluster will require proper authentication and precisely replicated configurations. For historical reasons, however, it will also work in very different ways depending on your particular operating system. In fact, at first glance, the hoops you'll need to jump through to get things going on pre-systemd Ubuntu 14.04 (or CentOS 6.6) machines might make it feel like you're operating in an entirely different world than on slightly more modern releases.

Part of the problem, of course, revolves around the differences between SysV/Upstart and systemd. But most of the confusion is due to the fact that, since Pacemaker version 1.1.8, the **crm** shell is, by and large, no longer installed by default (although it does still come with Pacemaker on Ubuntu 16.04), and has been replaced by **pcs**. You probably won't see too much of Corosync version 1.x even from repositories for older distributions like Ubuntu 14.04, but you should be aware that Corosync, in its 2.x releases, is able to act as its own quorum provider and, therefore, no longer requires a separate manager.

I'll describe the installation and configuration process with an eye to all the commonly used approaches.

Installation (CentOS 7)

First of all, you'll need at least two nodes configured to run some kind of application. Just for illustration purposes, I'll imagine that these will be web servers with Apache already installed.

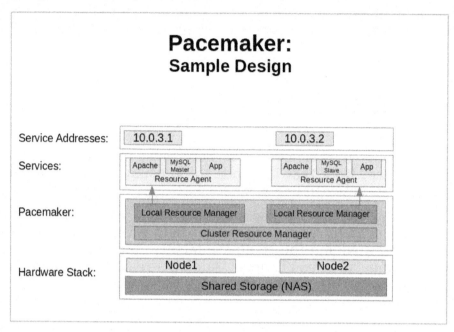

We'll eventually need to give Pacemaker - through a resource agent - access to the service status (Apache, in this example), so we'll create a **status.conf** file in the **/etc/httpd/conf.d/** directory of each node with the following contents:

```
<Location /server-status>
    SetHandler server-status
    Order Deny,Allow
    Deny from all
    Allow from 127.0.0.1
</Location>
```

Installation for the **pacemaker** and **pcs** packages on each node is from the regular yum repository

Since we're using the pcs shell, we'll need to start the pcs daemon and force it to launch on system boot:

```
# systemctl start pcsd
# systemctl enable pcsd
```

You'll see a new user on the system called hacluster. You should use **passwd** to give the user a password - just make sure you use the same password for hacluster on every node:

```
# passwd hacluster
```

You should add an entry to the **/etc/hosts** file on every cluster node assigning a host name (for either an IP or a DNS address) for every node in your cluster. The **hosts** files on my two-node cluster might look something like this:

```
127.0.0.1   localhost
10.0.3.1 MyNode1
10.0.3.2 MyNode2
```

The "MyNode" host names I use here must match the output of uname -n on each machine. Note that I happen to be using the local private IP addresses to communicate between nodes.

At this point, you should also make sure that your nodes can talk to each other (you might need to reboot your nodes before that happens). If you need to open firewall ports, adding the "high-availability" FirewallD rule to each node should cover all the ports you'll need. Adding --reload will load these rules for the current session.

```
# firewall-cmd --permanent --add-service=high-availability
# firewall-cmd --add-service=high-availability
# firewall-cmd --reload
```

Now it's time to authenticate between nodes to establish full communication. The cluster auth command only needs to be run on a single node. You'll be asked for a username (hacluster) and the password you previously gave it.

```
# pcs cluster auth MyNode1 MyNode2
```

You use cluster setup to generate and synchronize the Corosync configuration and assign it some name - "mycluster" in this example:

```
# pcs cluster setup --name mycluster MyNode1 MyNode2
```

You may need to manually bring Pacemaker up for the first time.

```
# systemctl start pacemaker
```

You're ready to go. Launch the cluster from pacemaker1:

```
# pcs cluster start --all
```

From each node, configure Pacemaker and Corosync to start on system boot (although this can also be done through the single command: **pcs cluster enable --all**):

```
# systemctl enable corosync
# systemctl enable pacemaker
```

To see what's happening, check the cluster status on each host:

```
# pcs status
```

If you happen to be running a simple cluster of only two nodes, then you might want to disable quorum requirements - because, after all, how could a *majority* of two nodes ever be healthy? For simplicity, you might also want to disable fencing by setting stonith to false:

```
# pcs property set no-quorum-policy=ignore
# pcs property set stonith-enabled=false
```

You can view your configuration using pcs config:

```
# pcs config
```

Installation: crm

Unlike pcs that handles corosync internally, crm works together with corosync. First of all, you'll need to install the **pacemaker** package. Then use corosync to generate an authentication key on your primary node:

```
# corosync-keygen
Corosync Cluster Engine Authentication key generator.
Gathering 1024 bits for key from /dev/random.
Press keys on your keyboard to generate entropy.
```

This will create a key file called authkey in the /etc/corosync/ directory, which you will then need to copy (using scp) to the /etc/corosync/ directory on each node. Make sure that the keys are owned by root and have 400 permissions.

```
# chmod 400 /etc/corosync/authkey
# chown root:root /etc/corosync/authkey
```

While many versions of Pacemaker will automatically generate and update your /etc/corosync/corosync.conf file, you will sometimes need to check it yourself. There should also be two example versions of the corosync.conf file called corosync.conf.example and corosync.conf.example.udpu. It's worth taking a look at those examples to see which one is most appropriate for your configuration. Here's what a working config file might look like:

```
totem {
        version: 2
        crypto_cipher: none
        crypto_hash: none
        interface {
                ringnumber: 0
                bindnetaddr: 192.168.0.102
                mcastport: 5405
                ttl: 1
        }
        transport: udpu
}
logging {
        fileline: off
        to_logfile: yes
        to_syslog: yes
        logfile: /var/log/corosync/corosync.log
        debug: off
        timestamp: on
        logger_subsys {
                subsys: QUORUM
                debug: off
        }
}
nodelist {
        node {
                ring0_addr: 192.168.200.16
                nodeid: 1
        }
        node {
                ring0_addr: 192.168.200.17
                nodeid: 2
        }
}
quorum {
        # Enable and configure quorum subsystem (default: off)
        #provider: corosync_votequorum
}
```

The key lines are bindnetaddr (which should contain the private IP address or accessible hostname of the local node), and the ring0_addr lines for each of the nodes in nodelist (which should contain the appropriate private IP address or hostname of that particular node). The nodelist section should be the same in the cluster.conf file on all nodes. The totem section defines the communication protocols Corosync will use, quorum will allow quorum checking (if we enable it) even with only two nodes running, and the logging section directs log messages to a unique corosync log file.

This example employs unicast mode (i.e., cluster messages will always be sent to a single node at a time). If you feel you can manage the added risk of a multicast architecture - including the added complexity of message authentication and group access control - then switching to multicasting mode can greatly increase the efficiency of your cluster communications. Identifying each node address as "ring0_addr" tells Corosync that these will be active nodes.

So that Pacemaker can communication with nodes through Corosync, you'll need to create a file called pcmk in the /etc/corosync/service.d/ directory of each node containing these lines:

```
service {
  name: pacemaker
  ver: 1
}
```

On pre-Systemd systems, you enable the Corosync service by editing the /etc/default/corosync file on all nodes, so that the value of START is yes:

```
START=yes
```

You're now ready to start Corosync. Run on all nodes, either:

```
# service corosync start
```

Or:

```
# systemctl start corosync
```

Verify that everything is working using:

```
# corosync-cmapctl | grep members
runtime.totem.pg.mrp.srp.members.1.config_version (u64) = 0
runtime.totem.pg.mrp.srp.members.1.ip     (str)    =    r(0)      ip
(192.168.0.102)
runtime.totem.pg.mrp.srp.members.1.join_count (u32) = 1
runtime.totem.pg.mrp.srp.members.1.status (str) = joined
runtime.totem.pg.mrp.srp.members.2.config_version (u64) = 0
runtime.totem.pg.mrp.srp.members.2.ip     (str)    =    r(0)      ip
(192.168.0.104)
runtime.totem.pg.mrp.srp.members.2.join_count (u32) = 1
runtime.totem.pg.mrp.srp.members.2.status (str) = joined
#
```

Again, make sure to run this on each node. This is obviously something that you will want to combine into a single script or template if you're planning to work with large numbers of nodes.

There are some useful Corosync monitoring tools. corosync-quorumtool will display the current status and settings of Pacemaker's quorum.

```
#  corosync-quorumtool
Quorum information
------------------
Date:              Sun Jun 26 19:47:26 2016
Quorum provider:   Not configured
Nodes:             0
Node ID:           0
Ring ID:           0
Quorate:           Yes
#
```

Of course, once you have some nodes running, you quorum information will look quite different. You can also edit the quorum voting settings using -v. corosync-cfgtool will display Corosync's "active parameters." And corosync-cmapctl can be used to access the object database.

Cluster Failover Management - crm

The crm tool allows close administration of your cluster. You can, for instance, enable STONITH using the configure property command like this:

```
# crm configure property stonith-enabled=true
```

You can list all the (many) available resource agents that can be activated using ra list lsb:

```
# crm ra list lsb
```

If I wanted to create a new resource - say, an IP address that I could later assign to individual nodes when access needs to be dynamically edited - I can configure a primitive. In this case, I'm calling my new address NewAddress, using the Open Cluster Framework class (ocf:heartbeat) as its resource agent, and assigning its parameters:

```
# crm configure primitive NewAddress ocf:heartbeat:IPaddr2 params
ip=192.168.0.150 cidr_netmask="24" op monitor interval="30s"
```

This will create an application resource agent for our Apache web server. (We will need to make sure that Apache isn't running on any of our nodes before adding the service to Pacemaker.) Notice how it points to the apache2 configuration file (for Debian-based machines, at least):

```
# crm configure primitive Apache ocf:heartbeat:apache params
configfile=/etc/apache2/apache2.conf op monitor interval="30s" op
start timeout="40s" op stop timeout="60s"
```

Now that we've got three additions to our cluster, let's use **crm configure show** to see how it all appears to Corosync:

```
# crm configure show
primitive Apache apache \
     params configfile="/etc/apache2/apache2.conf" \
     op monitor interval=30s \
     op start timeout=40s interval=0 \
     op stop timeout=60s interval=0
primitive NewAddress IPaddr2 \
     params ip=192.168.0.150 cidr_netmask=24 \
     op monitor interval=30s
property cib-bootstrap-options: \
     have-watchdog=false \
     dc-version=1.1.14-70404b0 \
     cluster-infrastructure=corosync \
     cluster-name=debian \
     stonith-enabled=true
#
```

crm resource show will display the current status of our new Pacemaker-managed resources:

```
# crm resource show
 NewAddress(ocf::heartbeat:IPaddr2):    Started
 Apache    (ocf::heartbeat:apache):     Started
#
```

You can start, stop, and remove resources pretty much the same way you created them. Here, we refer to our "Apache" resource by name:

```
# crm resource start Apache
# crm resource stop Apache
# crm configure delete Apache
```

The crm toolbox includes a number of command families, like crm_attribute (to query and modify a node's attributes), crm_shadow (to test configurations in a simulation sandbox), and crm_resource (to directly manage resources). Here are some examples:

This example will enable stonith on a node:

```
# crm_attribute --name stonith-enabled --update 1
```

And this one will set the default timeout value for all operations (besides those with their own pre-set timeouts):

```
# crm_attribute --type op_defaults --name timeout --update 20s
```

You can use crm_resource to query the status of a particular resource:

```
# crm_resource --locate --resource cluster1-rsc
```

If, for some reason, you need to prevent resources from running on a particular node, you might need some polite way to break the bad news to the cluster. crm_standby is that way. Running it with -G will query the current standby status of the current node.

```
# crm_standby -G
```

And -v followed by a value (either "on" or "off"), will change the standby status.

```
# crm_standby -v on
```

By the way, this can also be done on directly with crm using **standby nodename**.

Simply shutting down a node (using pcs cluster stop for instance) will not completely remove it from various cluster configurations. To finish that job, you can use crm_node, -R, and the name of the node.

```
# crm_node -R MyNode1
```

You can list all stonith-related devices on the system using stonith_admin.

```
# stonith_admin --list-installed
```

Perhaps, as it did in my case, stonith_admin returned a device called fence_pcmk. To display the parameters associated with the fence_pcmk, run:

```
# stonith_admin --metadata --agent fence_pcmk
```

You can test out a series of configuration changes without affecting your active cluster using **crm_shadow**:

```
# crm_shadow --create test
```

This will drop you into a sandboxed shell, where you can safely enter new directives.

You can also run **crm_simulate** to simulate cluster events and generate data representing the way the cluster will respond.

```
# crm_simulate --live-check -VVVVV --save-graph tmp.graph --save-dotfile tmp.dot
```

Typing crm by itself will drop you into a shell environment (identified by the **crm(live)#** prompt). The question mark (?) will list the commands and subshells accessible at this level, and typing an item from the list will execute it - or take you to a subshell. Typing status, for example, will return information on the current state of your cluster. Adding the **-Afn** flag will add Node and Migration data.

```
crm(live)# status
```

Updating information similar to Status will be displayed directly from your regular shell using **crm_mon**.

Templates

Pre-built Pacemaker profiles covering common scenarios in the form of templates are available to make easing into cluster administration a bit simpler. To see all the templates automatically installed along with your Pacemaker package, enter the crm shell, type **configure** and then **template** to drill down into the menu system, and then **list**.

```
# crm
crm(live)# configure
crm(live)configure# template
crm(live)configure template# list
Templates:
virtual-ip      gfs2-base      gfs2           sbd            filesystem
apache
ocfs2           clvm
crm(live)#
```

If you'd like to create a new configuration based on a particular template, you type **new**, followed by the name you'd like to give your configuration, and then the name of the template you want as your base.

```
crm(live)configure template# new new-conf apache
INFO: pulling in template apache
INFO: pulling in template virtual-ip
crm(live)configure template#
```

The shell will automatically pull in any necessary resources and create your configuration. Typing **list** once more will now show you the change.

```
crm(live)configure template# list
Templates:
virtual-ip      gfs2-base      gfs2           sbd            filesystem
apache
ocfs2           clvm

Configurations:
new-conf
crm(live)configure template#
```

While you've successfully created a new configuration, it probably won't be ready to use right out of the box. To see what's still left to do, running the **show** command followed by the name of your configuration will display any errors along with their line numbers.

```
crm(live)configure template# show new-conf
ERROR: 29: required parameter ip not set
ERROR: 80: required parameter configfile not set
crm(live)configure template#
```

To work with your conifiguration, simply type **edit** and the configuration name, and you'll be dropped into a special session of your default text editor (probably vi) that will include helpful instructions.

```
crm(live)configure template# edit new-conf
```

Here's what the first screen might look like:

```
# Configuration: conf-new

# Edit instructions:
#
# Add content only at the end of lines starting with '%%'.
# Only add content, don't remove or replace anything.
# The parameters following '%required' are not optional,
# unlike those following '%optional'.
# You may also add comments for future reference.

%name virtual-ip

# Copyright (C) 2009 Dejan Muhamedagic
#
# License: GNU General Public License (GPL)
# Virtual IP address
# This template generates a single primitive resource of type
IPaddr

%pfx virtual-ip
%required
```

Templates are represented within the cib.xml file between <template> tags. This example (taken from ClusterLabs documentation) defines the attributes, memory usage, and timeout value of a virtual machine and assigns the values to a template called vm-template:

```
<template      id="vm-template"      class="ocf"      provider="heartbeat"
type="Xen">
  <meta_attributes id="vm-template-meta_attributes">
          <nvpair    id="vm-template-meta_attributes-allow-migrate"
name="allow-migrate" value="true"/>
  </meta_attributes>
  <utilization id="vm-template-utilization">
        <nvpair  id="vm-template-utilization-memory"  name="memory"
value="512"/>
  </utilization>
  <operations>
     <op id="vm-template-monitor-15s" interval="15s" name="monitor"
timeout="60s"/>
          <op  id="vm-template-start-0"  interval="0"  name="start"
timeout="60s"/>
  </operations>
</template>
```

You could invoke your template within your cib.xml configuration in a number of ways, including as a constraint:

```
<constraints>
<rsc_colocation    id="vm-template-colo-base-rsc"    rsc="vm-template"
rsc-role="Started" with-rsc="base-rsc" score="INFINITY"/>
</constraints>
```

Resource Rules

Because most networks are made up of servers built with a range of hardware profiles, you might, by way of example, prefer that some particularly demanding tasks be performed only on your stronger machines. You can control the way your cluster assigns tasks using resource rules. A typical rule will appear within the <constraints> tags within the CIB (which, of course, is based on the **/var/lib/pacemaker/cib/cib.xml** file), and include an ID you choose to identify the rule (**id=""**), a resource value (**rsc=""**), a score giving the rule a particular weight (**score=""**), and sometimes a node to which the rule will apply (**node=""**).

You can define when and how a resource will be run on a node by giving the rule a numeric score. The score can be anywhere between -1,000,000 (also used as -INFINITY) and 1,000,000 (or INFINITY). The higher the score, the more likely the rule will be applied.

You can force a resource to be launched only on the same node as a different resource using **colocation**. If, say, the resource Apache is already running somewhere, you can use crm to force IPaddr2 to run only on that node (and, therefore, to not run at all if Apache isn't running anywhere) using this syntax:

```
# crm configure colocation IPaddr2 INFINITY: Apache
```

This is how this rule would then appear in your cib.xml file:

```
<rsc_colocation    id="colocate"    rsc="IPaddr2"    with-rsc="Apache"
score="INFINITY"/>
```

Anti-colocation forces a resource to run anywhere except the same node as a different specified resource. The "anti" effect is achieved through the use of -INFINITY.

```
# crm configure colocation IPaddr2 -INFINITY: Apache
```

...And here's how it would appear in cib.xml:

```
<rsc_colocation  id="anti-colocate"  rsc="IPaddr2"  with-rsc="Apache"
score=
"-INFINITY"/>
```

Constraints

Since software applications sometimes require preexisting resources, you might want to set the order by which resources on a node are launched. This next example makes it mandatory for Webserver to launch only after the Database is already running, and allows ("optional") IP to precede Webserver:

```
# crm configure order rule-name mandatory: IP Webserver
# crm configure order rule-name2 optional Database Webserver
```

...Which would show up in cib.xml like this:

```
<constraints>
<rsc_order        id="order-1"       first="IPaddr2"        then="Apache"
kind="Optional"/>
<rsc_order        id="order-2"       first="Database"       then="Apache"
kind="Mandatory" />
</constraints>
```

You can limit resources to specified nodes by applying location constraints. The following set of rules will explicitly permit your webserver resources to run on nodes MyNode1 and MyNode-3, and your database resources to run on MyNode-2 and MyNode-3. The score values tell Pacemaker that MyNode-1 is the preferred node for your webserver, and MyNode-2 is preferred for your database.

```
# crm configure location rule-name3 Apache 200: MyNode1
# crm configure location rule-name4 Apache 0: MyNode3
# crm configure location rule-name5 Database 200: MyNode2
# crm configure location rule-name6 Database 0: MyNode3
```

Which will appear this way in cib.xml:

```
<constraints>
        <rsc_location  id="loc-1"  rsc="Webserver"  node="MyNode1"
score="200"/>
        <rsc_location  id="loc-2"  rsc="Webserver"  node="MyNode3"
score="0"/>
         <rsc_location  id="loc-3"  rsc="Database"  node="MyNode2"
score="200"/>
        <rsc_location  id="loc-4"  rsc="Database"  node="MyNode-3"
score="0"/>
</constraints>
```

How you will constrain the use of your nodes depends on whether you want your cluster to be opt-in (i.e., by default *no* resource can run *anywhere*) or opt-out (by default *any* resource can run *anywhere*). Here's an example inspired by the ClusterLabs.org documentation pages. This attribute will create an opt-in cluster:

```
# crm_attribute --name symmetric-cluster --update false
```

Groups

If you've got two or more resources that need to live in the same location and that depend on each other (for instance, your application can only run on the same machine as a particular database that, say, is in Master mode), you can include them in a group. The resources you add to the group as primitives will load in the exact order in which they appear inside the <group> tags and, when the time comes, will unload in the exact opposite order.

```
<group id="shortcut">
        <primitive     id="Public-IP"    class="ocf"    type="IPaddr"
provider="heartbeat">
    <instance_attributes id="params-public-ip">
       <nvpair id="public-ip-addr" name="ip" value="192.0.2.2"/>
    </instance_attributes>
    </primitive>
    <primitive id="Email" class="lsb" type="exim"/>
</group>
```

At first, groups may appear to provide much of the same function as constraints; with both enforcing the behavior of specified resources in relation to others. However, relationships involving groups are more complete, meaning that an individual resource that fails will cause all subsequent resources in that group to stop. A colocation constraint, on the other hand, only governs the target resource's launch, but has no impact on other resources.

Cloning Resources

You can make a particular resource available on multiple cluster nodes by cloning it. This can make launching new nodes or even entire deployments much simpler, as you are effectively importing an active configuration. **Globally unique** clones will essentially act as independent copies of the original, assuming their own identities even on a single node. **Anonymous** clones (defined through a "false" value for their "globally-unique" field) will be identical in every way to the original. Here's how you might clone an Apache resource:

```
# crm configure clone Apache meta globally-unique="false"
```

And here's how it might then look in XML:

```
<clone id="apache-clone">
    <meta_attributes id="apache-clone-meta">
           <nvpair    id="apache-unique"    name="globally-unique"
value="false"/>
    </meta_attributes>
    <primitive id="apache" class="lsb" type="apache"/>
</clone>
```

...And here is how it might be referenced within a constraint:

```
<constraints>
        <rsc_location  id="clone-prefers-MyNode1"  rsc="apache-clone"
node="MyNode1" score="500"/>
            <rsc_colocation   id="stats-with-clone"   rsc="apache-stats"
with="apache-clone"/>
            <rsc_order  id="start-clone-then-stats"  first="apache-clone"
then="apache-stats"/>
</constraints>
```

Cluster Failover Management - pcs

Let's see how some of these functions can be executed using the pcs tool. Install the **pcs** package and then run **pcs status**:

```
# pcs status
```

Now let's use pcs to create the resources to run an Apache website while, at the same time, creating a new group called apache2group.

```
# pcs resource create my_fs Filesystem \
device="/dev/sda2" directory="/var/www/html" fstype="ext4" \
--group apache2group
```

We'll add a new virtual IP address with a unique IP address and associate it with the apache2group.

```
# pcs resource create VirtualIP IPaddr2 \
ip=192.168.0.151 cidr_netmask=24 --group apache2group
```

You can place a specified node on standby using **pcs standby nodename**, or place the whole cluster with the **-all** flag:

```
# pcs standby --all
```

Finally, I'll create the resource PublicSite and point it to a server-status file we create in the Apache root directory.

```
#    pcs    resource    create    PublicSite    apache    \
configfile="/etc/apache2/apache2.conf" \
statusurl="http://127.0.0.1/server-status" --group apache2group
```

This will create the launch order restraint we saw above in the crm section:

```
# pcs constraint order Database then Apache kind=Mandatory
# pcs constraint order IP then Apache kind=Optional
```

If one of your managed resources isn't loading the way you expect, you can run debug and the name of the resource and explore the output you get:

```
# pcs resource debug-start Apache
Operation start for Apache (ocf:heartbeat:apache) returned 0
 >  stderr: INFO: apache already running (pid 1556)
```

In this case, there was already a different Apache process running. Shutting it down using **kill 1556** should help.

The Cluster Information Base

As I wrote earlier, the Cluster Information Base is kept in a file in the **/var/lib/pacemaker/cib/** directory. However, you should never edit cib.xml directly, something that's guaranteed to cause some serious trouble. Instead, you can use the cibadmin command to copy the file contents to a temporary file, edit that file, and run cibadmin once again to save your edits to the original.

```
# cibadmin --query > temp.xml
# nano temp.xml
# cibadmin --replace --xml-file temp.xml
```

For more Pacemaker command line documentation details, visit the ClusterLabs web site:

clusterlabs.org/doc/en-US/Pacemaker/1.1/html-single/Pacemaker_Explained/

Resource Rules

Just as we saw above through crm, you can also create constraints using pcs:

```
# pcs constraint colocation add IPaddr2 with Apache INFINITY
```

And here is how we would apply an anti-colocation rule:

```
# pcs constraint colocation add IPaddr2 with Apache -INFINITY
```

Constraints

Here's how the resource **order** rules we illustrated earlier for crm would be applied using pcs:

```
# pcs constraint order Database then Apache kind=Mandatory
# pcs constraint order IP then Apache kind=Optional
```

And here are the **location** rules:

```
# pcs constraint location Webserver prefers MyNode1=200
# pcs constraint location Webserver prefers MyNode3=0
# pcs constraint location Database prefers MyNode2=200
# pcs constraint location Database prefers MyNode3=0
```

Command Cheat Sheet

Control PCS daemon	systemctl start pcsd
Open ports for Pacemaker	firewall-cmd --add-service=high-availability
Authenticate nodes	pcs cluster auth MyNode1 MyNode2
Generate configuration	pcs cluster setup --name mycluster MyNode1 MyNode2
Launch cluster	pcs cluster start --all
Generate keys	corosync-keygen
Safely edit cib.xml file	cibadmin --query > temp.xml
CRM	
Enable stonith	crm configure property stonith-enabled=true
List resource agents	crm ra list lsb
Configure resource	crm configure primitive NewAddress...
Show cluster resources	crm configure show
Stop a resource	crm resource stop Apache
Delete a resource	crm configure delete Apache
Query resource status	crm_resource --locate --resource cluster1-rsc
Place node on hold	crm_standby -G
Delete a node	crm_node -R MyNode1
List stonith devices	stonith_admin --list-installed
Use sandbox	crm_shadow --create test
Simulate configuration	crm_simulate --live-check --save-dotfile tmp.dot
List templates	crm configure template list
Create new configuration	crm configure template new myname apache
Edit configuration	crm configure template edit myname
Add colocation rule	crm configure colocation IPaddr2 INFINITY: Apache
Add constraint rule	crm configure order rule-name2 optional Database Webserver
PCS	

View status	pcs status
View configuration	pcs config
List resource agents	pcs resource agents
Place all nodes on hold	pcs standby --all
Disable stonith	pcs property set stonith-enabled=false
Create resource	pcs resource create my_fs Filesystem device="/dev/sda2"...
Delete a resource	pcs resource delete resourceid
Stop clusters	pcs cluster stop --all
Enable clusters	pcs cluster enable --all
Place node on standby	pcs cluster standby NodeName
Destroy cluster	pcs cluster destroy
Debug resource startup	pcs resource debug-start Apache
Add colocation rule	pcs constraint colocation add IPaddr2 with Apache INFINITY
Add constraint rule	pcs constraint order IP then Apache kind=Optional

Resources:
Project Home:	clusterlabs.org/wiki/Pacemaker
Documentation:	clusterlabs.org/doc/

Test Yourself

1. Which of the following is correct?

a) Corosync provides coordination and communication services for Pacemaker deployments

b) Pacemaker provides coordination and communication services for Corosync deployments

c) Heartbeat provides coordination and duplication services for Corosync deployments

d) Heartbeat provides duplication for Pacemaker

2. What is the primary task of the Cluster Information Base (CIB)?

a) Calculate new cluster configurations

b) Coordinate communication between cluster nodes

c) Maintain and synchronize cluster and node status data

d) Assign tasks to resource agents

3. The /etc/httpd/conf.d/status.conf file on a Pacemaker node running Apache serves what function?

a) Tells Apache to forward any incoming requests form a Pacemaker resource agent

b) Forces Apache to reload only after the Pacemaker service has started after boot

c) Permits the resource agent to check on the status of the Apache service

d) Forces Pacemaker to reload only after the Apache service has started after boot

4. What is the name of the user that's created during Pacemaker installation?

a) pcsd

b) cluster

c) nodeagent

d) hacluster

5. Within the context of Pacemaker resource rules, which of these best describes the function of a constraint?

a) A constraint is a section within a cib.xml file that determines a resource agent's priority

b) A constraint is a section within a cib.xml file whose contents define resource agent behavior

c) A constraint is a section within a cib.xml file that determines where a resource agent may run

d) A constraint is a section within a cib.xml file whose contents limit the power of resource agents

Answer Key: 1:b,2:c,3:c,4:d,5:c

10. Enterprise Resources

LPIC-304 Exam Objective 334.4

Red Hat Enterprise Linux High Availability Add-On

Besides the regular command line tools - some of which we've already discussed at length - the Red Hat Enterprise Linux High Availability Add-On provides alternate administration options – whether or not you choose to work through Pacemaker. **Conga** is a browser-based GUI interface (installed through "yum install luci") for installing, configuring, and managing the add-on. More recently a separate browser-based interface called pcs-gui has become available as a frontend for the pcs command line utility.

In addition, Red Hat provides the Ruby-based PCSD HTTPS browser-based GUI management tool that runs using port 2224.

SUSE Linux Enterprise High Availability Extension

SUSE's extension also offers a GUI administration tool (called **YaST**) as well as a browser based console - **HA Web Konsole** (Hawk) - which makes administration from non-Linux computers possible. The extension also includes enhanced features like a large library of pre-built resource agents.

11. High Availability Cluster Storage: DRBD / cLVM

LPIC-304 Exam Objective 335.1

Installation and Configuration

DRBD Status

DRBD Architectural Models (cLVM)

As we've seen, cluster management and load balancing - with all their replication and system-wide intelligence - provide significant benefits for the reliability of our application servers. But the data on which your servers rely also deserves the same kind of tender care and feeding. The Linux Distributed Replicated Block Device (DRBD) has long been a useful tool for just this purpose. And since 2009 (release 2.6.33), it's been included in the Linux kernel out of the box.

DRBD stores your data on DRBD devices mounted on partitions on one or more nodes. The partitions are synchronized with each other so that any files created or updated on the active node are automatically available in their current form across the system. Once integrated into a cluster management system like Pacemaker, data is protected by a failover utility which can designate any one node as primary and then, if it fails, fence it and appoint a healthy node as primary in its place.

If you plan to allow cluster nodes to share each other's resources, you'll need to make your data uniformly accessible to multiple servers on the cluster without exposing them to the risk of corruption. You do this by configuring some kind of cluster file system to ensure that all data stores are properly synchronized and remain coherent. The cLVM daemon (cLVMD) can help by synchronizing LVM metadata.

Installation and Configuration

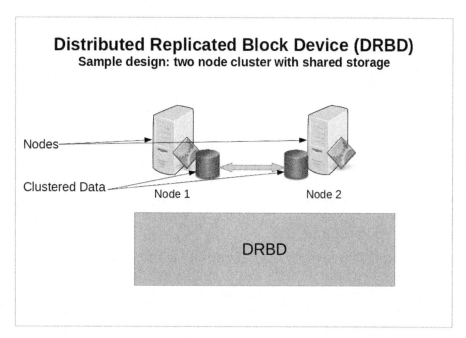

First, you'll have to prepare at least two servers to act as DRBD nodes. Make sure that each of them has an unused and unformatted partition of about the same size. While the drbdadm tool can edit partitions, you might be more comfortable using the Linux Logical Volume Manager (LVM) to get things exactly the way you want them.

List all the block devices recognized by your system to identify the unused partition you will be using.

```
$ lsblk
```

We'll assume that the one we're after is /dev/sda5.

Now install the DRBD package (**drbd8-utils**) - which controls the drbd kernel module that comes with the Linux kernel - along with **clvm**.

The drbd package will include the drbdadm administration tool, which we're going to be using from the command line. It will also install drbdsetup (to manage the relationships between DRBD devices and their underlying block devices) and drbdmeta (for managing meta data storage). It's unusual to call either of those two tools directly, as they're normally meant to be invoked as part of processes run by the drbdadm front end.

DRBD Configuration

With DRBD installed, you should focus on the /etc/drbd.d/ directory which, by default, should contain a file called global_common.conf. The active elements of that file might look like this:

```
global {
  usage-count yes;
}
common {
  net {
    protocol C;
  }
}
```

If the value of **usage-count** is "yes" then data will be sent to the DRBD's online usage counter to help them track how many times the software is installed. The **protocol** value has more immediate implications. There are three possible protocols you can choose from: A, B, and – yes! - C. These protocols are also known as replication modes.

Protocol A provides asynchronous replication in which completed writes to the local primary node are considered finished even before the replication to secondary nodes is confirmed. There is therefore a risk that changes committed immediately before a forced failover might be lost.

Protocol B uses memory synchronous replication where local write is considered complete only once the replication packet makes it to the secondary nodes. Data loss can still occur in memory synchronous replication if all nodes should experience a simultaneous power failure while write operations are still finalizing.

Protocol C is the synchronous replication protocol that requires writes to all disks to be confirmed complete before an operation is closed. At this point, a full failure of any single node will definitely not result in a permanent data loss. Protocol C is by far the most-used method in production deployments.

Before anything good can happen on a DRBD system, you'll need to create an identical .res resource configuration file within the /etc/drbd.d/ directory of **each** node. The files will establish your network protocols, and identify and define each node along with its own configuration. You should name the file after the value of "resource" within the file itself. In our case, that will be r0.res. Here's how it might look for a simple, two-node system:

```
resource r0 {
    net {
        protocol C;
        cram-hmac-alg sha1;
        shared-secret "secret";
    }
    disk {
        resync-rate 10M;
    }
    on drbd1 {
        volume 0 {
            device      minor 1;
            disk        /dev/sda5;
            meta-disk internal;
        }
        address   10.0.3.67:7789;
    }
    on drbd2 {
        volume 0 {
            device      minor 1;
            disk        /dev/sda5;
            meta-disk internal;
        }
        address   10.0.3.88:7789;
    }
}
```

Protocol, as we've seen, can take values of A, B, and C; **shared-secret** is used for peer authentication; and **resync-rate** (the maximum bandwidth allowed for a device's background synchronization) is measured in MB/second. The hostname in the "**on**" section (drbd1 and drbd2 in my case) should be the same as the Linux host name of each of the actual nodes. You can, of course, use uname -n on a node to display the hostname. The **device** "minor" value will be appended to the partition designation used by the node file system (which will probably be something like /dev/drbd1). "**disk**" is the local node's original designation for the partition we will provide. In my case, that would have been /dev/sda5 in each node.

Any value which is not explicitly set in the .res file will follow the DRBD defaults, many of which are included in the /etc/drbd.d/global_common.conf file.

With the partitions and their configurations set for each node, we're ready to initialize our meta data storage. On each node, run create-md against our resource name ("r0" in this case).

```
# drbdadm create-md r0
initializing activity log
NOT initializing bitmap
Writing meta data...
New drbd meta data block successfully created.
#
```

...where r0 is the name of the resource file in /etc/drbd.d.

Start up the DRBD daemon on both nodes in the usual way:

```
# systemctl start drbd
```

drbdadm up can be used as a shorthand command for loading nodes.

Let's take a look at the daemon status:

```
# systemctl status drbd
● drbd.service - LSB: Control drbd resources.
   Loaded: loaded (/etc/init.d/drbd; bad; vendor preset: enabled)
   Active: active (exited) since Tue 2016-06-28 15:43:15 EDT; 2min
16s ago
     Docs: man:systemd-sysv-generator(8)
   Process: 19090 ExecStart=/etc/init.d/drbd  start  (code=exited,
status=0/SUCCESS

Jun 28 15:42:44 drbd1 drbd[19090]:  * Starting DRBD resources
Jun 28 15:42:44 drbd1 drbd[19090]: [
Jun 28 15:42:44 drbd1 drbd[19090]:       create res: r0
Jun 28 15:42:44 drbd1 drbd[19090]:     prepare disk: r0
Jun 28 15:42:44 drbd1 drbd[19090]:      adjust disk: r0
Jun 28 15:42:44 drbd1 drbd[19090]:       adjust net: r0
Jun 28 15:42:44 drbd1 drbd[19090]: ]
Jun 28 15:43:15 drbd1 drbd[19090]: WARN: stdin/stdout is not a TTY;
using /dev/c
Jun 28 15:43:15 drbd1 drbd[19090]:     ...done.
Jun  28  15:43:15  drbd1  systemd[1]:  Started  LSB:  Control  drbd
resources..
```

You will now have to designate one of your nodes as primary. You might first need to manually remove other nodes from the running so the poor, hard working daemon on your primary node doesn't become confused. You do that by running drbdadm with the invalidate argument on each secondary node.

```
# drbdadm invalidate r0
```

Now, back on the primary node, set the node as "primary".

```
# drbdadm -- --overwrite-data-of-peer primary r0
```

Note: if this command fails with a timeout, you can run it again with the **connect** argument to complete the connection.

You will need to give the partition on your **primary** node (which should now be called something like /dev/drbd1) a file system, and mount it to an empty mount directory:

```
# mkfs.ext3 /dev/drbd1
mke2fs 1.42.13 (17-May-2015)
Creating filesystem with 2441132 4k blocks and 610800 inodes
Filesystem UUID: 88bbaac8-aa48-470c-9e3f-1856fddacec3
Superblock backups stored on blocks:
     32768, 98304, 163840, 229376, 294912, 819200, 884736, 1605632
Allocating group tables: done
Writing inode tables: done
Creating journal (32768 blocks): done
Writing superblocks and filesystem accounting information:
done
# mount /dev/drbd1 /srv
```

Your DRBD data store should be up and running.

Three-Way Replication

You can build remote replication into your DRBD system by stacking another DRBD resource layer on top of the layer you're using for your cluster deployment. This new layer will connect to and replicate the data from your primary node, and then regularly back the data up to a remote location through an automated process like a cron job. For this connection, you would normally use DRBD Protocol A.

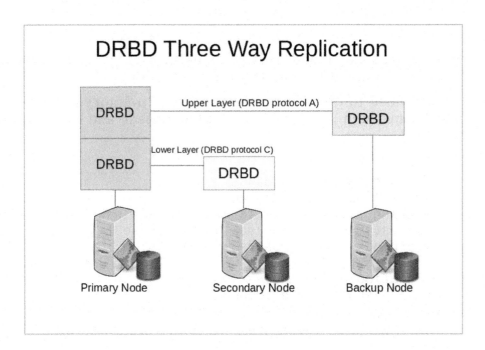

Dual-primary Mode

When access to your public-facing resources is managed by a load balancer, your cluster needs a way to manage multiple primary nodes - each one of which could be called to act as primary at any time.

You can enable dual-primary mode through the resource configuration file in the /etc/drbd.d/ directory (called r0.res in our example) by adding **allow-two-primaries;** to the **net** section of the file. Adding a **startup** section with the value **become-primary-on both;** will cause the resource to startup as primary on system startup:

```
startup {
   become-primary-on both;
}
```

For the changes to take effect, you'll need to disconnect and then connect your resource by running these commands on both nodes:

```
# drbdadm disconnect r0.res
# drbdadm connect r0.res
```

DRBD Status

At any time, you can view the status of DRBD from any node by reading the /proc/drbd file. From a secondary node, it might look like this:

```
$ cat /proc/drbd
version: 8.4.5 (api:1/proto:86-101)
srcversion: D496E56BBEBA8B1339BB34A

 1: cs:SyncTarget ro:Secondary/Primary ds:Inconsistent/UpToDate C
r-----
     ns:0 nr:7948348 dw:7948348 dr:0 al:0 bm:0 lo:0 pe:0 ua:0 ap:0
ep:1 wo:f oos:1816180
     [===============>....] sync'ed: 81.5% (1772/9532)M
     finish: 0:00:56 speed: 32,120 (35,800) want: 38,600 K/sec
```

That ro:Secondary/Primary line would be correct on a secondary node. This, on the other hand, is what we'd hope to see on the primary node:

```
$ cat /proc/drbd
version: 8.4.5 (api:1/proto:86-101)
srcversion: D496E56BBEBA8B1339BB34A

 1: cs:SyncSource ro:Primary/Secondary ds:UpToDate/Inconsistent C
r---n-
     ns:9261552 nr:0 dw:0 dr:9264200 al:0 bm:0 lo:0 pe:3 ua:1 ap:0
ep:1 wo:f oos:505520
     [==================>..] sync'ed: 94.9% (492/9532)M
     finish: 0:00:11 speed: 42,876 (36,308) K/sec
```

Notice the reversed order of "ro:Primary/Secondary"

If, on the other hand, you would see **Secondary/Secondary** or **Secondary/Unknown**, it could mean that DRBD is still getting things running after a start up, or that there's something wrong with either your configuration or one of your partitions.

Statistics associated with a particular resource can be displayed using something like:

```
# drbdadm status myresource --statistics
```

Modern DRBD releases also provide information about your nodes through drbd-overview (this example was run from the primary node):

```
# drbd-overview
1:r0/0  Connected Primary/Secondary UpToDate/UpToDate
#
```

To test your system, create some files within the file system on the primary drive, unmount the partition, demote that node down to secondary, promote your secondary node to primary, mount that secondary partition to a mount point on that node, and take a look at the files you created on the other node.

From the original primary node (drbd1):

```
# umount /srv
# drbdadm secondary r0
```

From the node that I called drbd2:

```
# drbdadm primary r0
# mount /dev/drbd1 /srv
```

DRBD Pacemaker Integration

It's a common practice to expose a DRBD data store to the nodes of a Pacemaker cluster. In such a case, you will need to disable the DRBD daemon, and let the Open Cluster Framework (OCF) resource agent take over.

```
# systemctl disable drbd
drbd.service is not a native service, redirecting to systemd-sysv-
install
Executing /lib/systemd/systemd-sysv-install disable drbd
insserv: warning: current start runlevel(s) (empty) of script
`drbd' overrides LSB defaults (2 3 4 5).
insserv: warning: current stop runlevel(s) (0 1 2 3 4 5 6) of
script `drbd' overrides LSB defaults (0 1 6).
#
```

The OCF agent installs as /usr/lib/ocf/resource.d/linbit/drbd and can be configured using the crm shell.

You should first set DRBD to automatically make itself primary if necessary by adding the **auto-promote yes;** line to the **common** section of the /etc/drbd.d/global_common.conf file on each node. Then (after installing Pacemaker and confirming that it's properly configured and running on all your nodes), using Pacemaker's crm tool, you should create appropriate resources, group them together, and point them to your DRBD mountpoint.

Using the crm shell, that might look something like this:

```
crm(live)# configure
crm(live)configure#      primitive   drbd0   ocf:heartbeat:drbd   params
drbd_resource=drbd0 op monitor role=Master interval=59s timeout=30s
op monitor role=Slave interval=60s timeout=30s
crm(live)configure# ms ms-drbd0 drbd0 meta clone-max=2 notify=true
globally-unique=false target-role=stopped
crm(live)configure# commit
crm(live)configure# show
node 2130706433: drbd2
xml    <primitive    id="drbd0"    class="ocf"    provider="heartbeat"
type="drbd"> \
  <instance_attributes id="drbd0-instance_attributes"> \
        <nvpair  name="drbd_resource"  value="drbd0"  id="drbd0-
instance_attributes-drbd_resource"/> \
  </instance_attributes> \
  <operations> \
    <op name="monitor" role="Master" interval="59s" timeout="30s"
id="drbd0-monitor-59s"/> \
     <op name="monitor" role="Slave" interval="60s" timeout="30s"
id="drbd0-monitor-60s"/> \
  </operations> \
</primitive>
ms ms-drbd0 drbd0 \
    meta  clone-max=2  notify=true  globally-unique=false  target-
role=stopped
property cib-bootstrap-options: \
    have-watchdog=false \
    dc-version=1.1.14-70404b0 \
    cluster-infrastructure=corosync \
    cluster-name=debian \
    stonith-enabled=false
```

CLVMd

If more than one of your cluster's nodes will be simultaneously accessing your
DRBD data (and LVM is installed on the device), then you'll need to install the
LVM extension, CLVM (Clustered Logical Volume Manager), which is run by the
CLVMd daemon. CLVM performs critical access control functions to lock
partitions while they're being configured and to ensure that writes performed by
cluster resources don't create dangerous conflicts.

You'll need to run the CLVMd daemon in **each** cluster node so it can properly
receive timely LVM metadate updates. You can start the service using:

```
# systemctl start clvmd
```

...and ensure that it will load on reboot with:

```
# systemctl enable clvmd
```

Note: since CentOS 7, the CLVM daemon is started through Pacemaker only.

CLVM works just the same on clusters as its LVM cousin works on single machines. It's important to remember that all the resources you will include must be accessible to all the nodes in your cluster. Therefore, the physical volumes you will include in your volume group must all be reachable by each node.

Thus, volume groups created on a cluster node using **vgcreate** will be invisible to all cluster nodes unless you add the **-c** flag to the vgcreate command.

You can control resource locking (to prevent multiple users trying to write changes at the same time) through the "**locking_type =**" line in the **/etc/lvm/lvm.conf** file on each node. Assigning a value of "3" applies built-in clustered locking through the CLVM daemon.

This example shows how you might turn control of CLVM over to Pacemaker so it can apply constraints like colocation to your volumes:

```
# pcs resource create dlm ocf:pacemaker:controld op monitor on-
fail=fence clone ordered=true
# pcs resource create clvmd ocf:heartbeat:clvm op monitor on-
fail=fence clone ordered=true
# pcs constraint order start dlm-clone then clvmd-clone
# pcs constraint colocation add clvmd-clone with dlm-clone
```

Command Cheat Sheet

DRBD global settings	/etc/drbd.d/global_common.conf
DRBD resource config file	/etc/drbd.d/r0.res
LVM configuration file	/etc/lvm/lvm.conf
Initialize meta data storage	drbdadm create-md r0
Demote local node from primary	drbdadm invalidate r0
Promote local node to primary	drbdadm primary r0
View DRBD status	cat /proc/drbd

Resources:	
Project Home:	drbd.org/en/
Documentation:	drbd.org/en/doc/users-guide-90

Test Yourself

1. What role does the cLVM daemon play in DRBD high availability cluster storage?

a) Organizes distributed file system architectures

b) Synchronizes kernel-level communication with individual nodes

c) Synchronizes kernel-level communication with the DRBD daemon

d) Ensures safe access to data by multiple cluster nodes

2. Which DRBD tool specifically manages relationships between DRBD devices?

a) drbdadm

b) drbdmeta

c) drbdctrl

d) drbdconf

3. Which of these replication protocols uses memory synchronous replication?

a) Protocol A

b) Protocol B

c) Protocol C

d) Protocol D

4. Where does the .res DRBD configuration file go?

a) /etc/drbd.d/ on each node

b) /etc/ on each node

c) /etc/drbd.d/ on the Pacemaker Designated Coordinator

d) /etc/ on the Pacemaker Designated Coordinator

5. What's the best way to get DRBD status information?

a) cat /proc/drbd

b) drbdadm status --statistics

c) drbdadm myresource --status

d) drbdadm status myresource --statistics

Answer Key: 1:d,2:a,3:b,4:a,5:d

12. Clustered File Systems

LPIC-304 Exam Objective 335.2

OCFS (Oracle Cluster File System)

GFS2 (Global File System 2)

Pacemaker Integration

Other Storage Resources

Introduction

Among other things, a file system represents the contents of a block device to the user interface in a way that simplifies file identification and access. Since, on multi-user systems like Linux, there's always the chance that a single file might be accessed by two users at the same time, there need to be controls to prevent data corruption. This becomes more complicated when you add users of cluster nodes to the users already logged in locally.

A clustered file system provides cluster nodes with controlled access to shared storage with the help of a distributed lock manager (DLM). When configured appropriately, a storage cluster can allow clients with write permissions to edit its contents while preventing access when necessary to protect the data from potentially disastrous conflicts. As each node is constantly aware of its peers, a local failure can also be quickly isolated from the rest of a cluster through fencing, again, reducing the risk of data corruption.

Clustered systems - since they can be hosted on block storage devices - are particularly well suited for networks with high numbers of data nodes where transfer rates can be significantly higher than those found on more traditional NFS (Network File System) arrangements. A cluster file system - like Oracle's OCFS2 - that makes use of a simpler, distributed lock manager, can maintain system-wide data integrity while very quickly self-correcting for downed nodes or other interruptions.

The ideal cluster file system should be POSIX-compliant and provide effective transparency of access (where authorized). It should also handle concurrency, failure-recovery, and scalability, and allow free access between operating systems.

OCFS2 (Oracle Cluster File System)

Since the release of Version Two of Oracle's OCFS cluster file system with its support for POSIX, it has become far simpler to deploy clusters running on Linux server distributions besides Oracle Linux and SLES. With that, the significant performance advantages of OCFS2 across a wide range of workload types with shared storage (like multi-primary-dbrd, for instance) are now broadly accessible.

The nodes on an OCFS2 cluster are peers, so identical configuration files should be present on each node. On Debian-based systems, you'll want to install the **ocfs2-tools** package (which sets up the O2CB cluster stack). If you're using Red Hat or CentOS (or Oracle Linux), things are a bit more complicated: since moving to their GFS system, Red Hat no longer supports OCFS2. If, for some reason, you absolutely need to work with CentOS, guides to adding the appropriate repositories and getting OCFS2 running on a RHEL machine are available online.

OCFS2: Pacemaker Administration

You will often want to install OCFS2, but let Pacemaker manage your storage for you. You would first need to create primitive resources for both DLM (which must have already be running on all cluster nodes) and O2CB, and enable them by way of a cloned resource group . That might look something like this (except for CentOS 7 and later, as the ocfs2 provider is no longer available):

```
# crm configure primitive p_controld ocf:pacemaker:controld
# crm configure primitive p_o2cb ocf:ocfs2:o2cb
# crm configure group g_ocfs2mgmt p_controld p_o2cb
# crm configure clone cl_ocfs2mgmt g_ocfs2mgmt meta interleave=true
```

The Pacemaker ocf:heartbeat:Filesystem resource agent can be used to have Pacemaker control OCFS2 file systems:

```
# crm configure primitive fs_ocfs2 ocf:heartbeat:Filesystem \
  params device="/dev/drbd/by-res/ocfs2" directory="/srv/ocfs2" \
        fstype="ocfs2" options="rw,noatime"
# crm configure clone cl_fs_ocfs2 fs_ocfs2
```

These constraints can be added to force your resources to load together:

```
# crm configure order o_ocfs2 \
    ms_drbd_ocfs2:promote cl_ocfs2mgmt:start cl_fs_ocfs2:start
# crm configure colocation c_ocfs2 cl_fs_ocfs2 \
    cl_ocfs2mgmt ms_drbd_ocfs2:Master
```

OCFS2: Direct Administration

Should you choose to let the O2CB stack manage your OCFS2 storage resources directory, you set up the clustered partitions on each node through these two files:

- **/etc/ocfs2/cluster.conf** - which controls the layout of the cluster; mapping all of its resources, and...

- **/etc/sysconfig/oc2cb** (or, on some systems, **/etc/default/oc2b**), which defines the connection timeout policies.

Here is a simple example of a cluster.conf file for a three-cluster setup:

```
cluster:
        node_count = 3
        name = webcluster
node:
        ip_port = 7777
        ip_address = 192.168.0.107
        number = 7
        name = node7
        cluster = webcluster
node:
        ip_port = 7777
        ip_address = 192.168.0.106
        number = 6
        name = node6
        cluster = webcluster
node:
        ip_port = 7777 /usr/share/doc/ocfs2-tools/examples/
        ip_address = 192.168.0.110
        number = 10
        name = node10
        cluster = webcluster
```

Note how each node is identified by its host name (which must be identical to the content of its **/etc/hostname** file), and by its unique network IP address. Note also how each node in this example is a member of the same "webcluster" cluster.

Here's an example of the o2cb file which, depending on your Linux distribution, should be generated and modified either by running:

```
# service o2cb configure
```

or

```
# dpkg-reconfigure ocfs2-tools
```

```
# O2CB_ENABLED: 'true' means to load the driver on boot.
O2CB_ENABLED=false

# O2CB_BOOTCLUSTER: If not empty, the name of a cluster to start.
O2CB_BOOTCLUSTER=ocfs2

# O2CB_HEARTBEAT_THRESHOLD: Iterations before a node is considered
dead.
O2CB_HEARTBEAT_THRESHOLD=31

# O2CB_IDLE_TIMEOUT_MS: Time in ms before a network connection is
considered dead.
O2CB_IDLE_TIMEOUT_MS=30000

# O2CB_KEEPALIVE_DELAY_MS: Max. time in ms before a keepalive
packet is sent.
O2CB_KEEPALIVE_DELAY_MS=2000

# O2CB_RECONNECT_DELAY_MS: Min. time in ms between connection
attempts.
O2CB_RECONNECT_DELAY_MS=2000
```

To make sure that the system resets itself when necessary, you should enable kernel panic (before starting the stack) by adding these two lines to the **/etc/sysctl.conf** file:

```
kernel.panic = 30
kernel.panic_on_oops=1
```

Command Line Administration

Assuming you've decided to run OCFS2 from the command line (and not through Pacemaker), you can start and stop the service using the service command (or, alternatively, **systemctl**):

```
# service o2cb online
# service o2cb offline
```

From Pacemaker, startup would look like this:

```
# crm resource start resource_name_ocfs2
```

To get started setting up a new node to join a cluster, you should ideally prepare storage space on one or more separate partitions. You will then need to format (or, in cluster terms, initialize) your partitions with mkfs.ocfs2. Assuming that the partition you'd like to format is /dev/sda4 and you'd like it to have default values, you would run this:

```
# mkfs.ocfs2 -b 4K -C 32K -N 3 -L volumename /dev/sda4
mkfs.ocfs2 0.99.15-BETA16
Filesystem label=volumename
Block size=4096 (bits=12)
Cluster size=32768 (bits=15)
Volume size=21474820096 (655359 clusters) (5242872 blocks)
21 cluster groups (tail covers 10239 clusters, rest cover 32256
clusters)
Journal size=33554432
Initial number of node slots: 3
Creating bitmaps: done
Initializing superblock: done
Writing system files: done
Writing superblock: done
Writing lost+found: done
mkfs.ocfs2 successful
#
```

-L specifies a volume label to make it easier to identify it among your other resources. -N sets the initial number of node slots.

You can also add the **--cluster-stack** flag to specify a non-default (i.e., non-o2cb) stack. Possible values are pcmk (Pacemaker) and cman.

Once you've started your O2CB cluster, you can mount your formatted partition to an empty directory somewhere on the node. When O2CB is online, the mount command will actually execute mount.ocfs2.

```
# mount /dev/sda4 /home/directoryname
```

Management

Assuming the cluster is online (so it can confirm that the local resource is not currently in use by a network server), you can change many resource parameters including the size of a volume using **tunefs.ocfs2 --volume-size**, and the number of nodes allowed to concurrently mount a volume using **tunefs.ocfs2 --node-slots <number-of-node-slots> <drive path>**.

The special O2CB version of fsck will detect disks and fix disk errors - assuming, again, that the cluster is online:

```
# fsck.ocfs2 -f /dev/sda4
```

You can use **mounted** to detect and report details of all of your OCFS2 volumes:

```
# mounted.ocfs2 -d
# mounted.ocfs2 -f
```

The o2info tool, when run against an OCFS2 volume, will return comprehensive information even for users without root privileges. **o2image** will create an image file of an OCFS2 file system device metadata. When used with **debugfs.ocfs2**, the image file can be helpful for performance and failure analysis.

Oracle itself strongly recommends that you use their GUI console to create and apply the cluster to all of your nodes. You can install the **ocfs2console** package on a Debian machine. Running **ocfs2console** from the command line (or via a remote ssh -X session) will launch the GUI console:

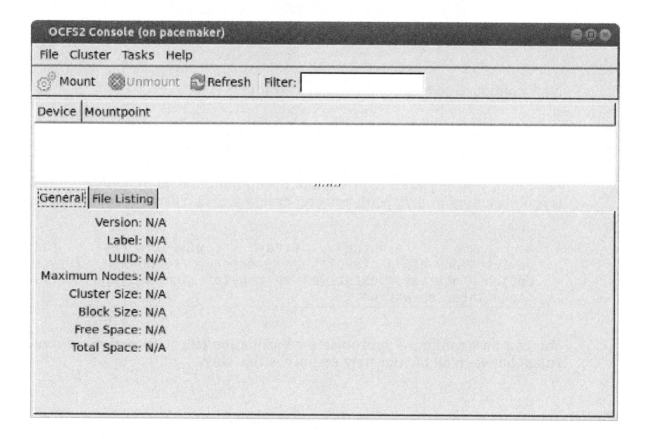

Resources:
Project Home: oss.oracle.com/projects/ocfs2/
Documentation: oss.oracle.com/projects/ocfs2/documentation/

GFS2 (Global File System 2)

GFS2: Pacemaker Administration

Assuming that you've got at least two working and connected nodes running Pacemaker on CentOS 7, here's how you can install, configure, and launch a GFS2 environment on top of Pacemaker. Use yum to install the utils and Distributed Lock Manager (DLM) packages on both nodes:

```
# yum install -y gfs2-utils dlm
```

Next, you can create clone resources for both DLM and CLVMD:

```
# pcs resource create dlm ocf:pacemaker:controld op monitor
interval=30s on-fail=fence clone interleave=true ordered=true
# pcs resource create clvmd ocf:heartbeat:clvm op monitor
interval=30s on-fail=fence clone interleave=true ordered=true
```

Now configure co-location for those resources:

```
# pcs constraint colocation add clvmd-clone with dlm-clone
```

Assuming you've got an LVM volume group mounted to /dev/dfsvg/gfsvol1 and a target directory of /kvmpool, you can create a gfs2 cluster resource with this:

```
# pcs resource create gfsvolfs_res Filesystem
device="/dev/gfsvg/gfsvol1" directory="/kvmpool" fstype="gfs2"
options="noatime,nodiratime" op monitor interval=10s on-fail=fence
clone interleave=true
```

You can now configure appropriate coordination (through **order** and **colocation** rules) between all of your new resources this way:

```
# pcs constraint order start clvmd-clone then gfsvolfs_res-clone
# pcs  constraint  colocation  add  gfsvolfs_res-clone   with  clvmd-
clone
```

Finally, this will set your cluster to freeze if there is no quorum:

```
# pcs property set no-quorum-policy=freeze
```

GFS2: Direct Administration

GFS2 works through a **cluster.conf** file in the **/etc/cluster/** directory on each node. If you choose to manage your storage directly (as opposed to through Pacemaker) a simple, two-node cluster.conf file might look like this:

```xml
<?xml version="1.0"?>
<cluster config_version="3" name="test-gfs-cluster">
<fence_daemon post_fail_delay="0" post_join_delay="3"/>
  <clusternodes>
    <clusternode name="node1" nodeid="1" votes="1">
      <fence>
        <method name="scsi">
          <device name="scsi_1" key="1"/>
        </method>
      </fence>
      <unfence>
        <device name="scsi_1" key="1" action="on"/>
      </unfence>
    </clusternode>
    <clusternode name="node2" nodeid="2" votes="1">
      <fence>
        <method name="scsi">
          <device name="scsi_1" key="2"/>
        </method>
      </fence>
      <unfence>
        <device name="scsi_1" key="2" action="on"/>
      </unfence>
    </clusternode>
  </clusternodes>
  <cman expected_votes="1" two_node="1" broadcast="yes">
  </cman>
  <fencedevices>
                <fencedevice    agent="fence_scsi"    name="scsi_1"
devices="/dev/mapper/mpathbp1"/>
  </fencedevices>
  <rm>
    <failoverdomains/>
    <resources/>
  </rm>
</cluster>
```

Since this cluster has only two nodes, you will have to allow a quorum ("expected_votes=") of 1 - rather than the usual majority of nodes (see chapter seven, High Availability Concepts and Theory). The **fence_scsi** agent will require its own partition (which must be created manually).

At this point, using Red Hat's (proprietary) graphic interface, if you're satisfied with your new configuration, clicking on the "Send to Cluster" button will propagate your **cluster.conf** file to the **/etc/cluster/** directory of each node you've included. Again, under normal conditions it's probably a good idea to work through this GUI but, nevertheless, the LPIC-3 304 exam expects you to be familiar with managing your clusters through the command line, so that's where we'll focus most of our attention.

Install the GFS2 utilities from the **gfs2-utils** package. On RHEL or CentOS (which is probably where you're going to be running GFS2), you can simplify the process by running:

```
# yum install gfs* lvm2
```

After creating a logical volume using LVM, you will need to create a GFS2 file system for it using mkfs.gfs2.

```
# mkfs.gfs2 -p lock_dlm -t MyCluster:mygfs2 -j 2 /dev/vg0/mygfs2
```

The value given to -p (*lock_dlm*) specifies which distributed lock manager protocol you want to use (lock_dlm is necessary for shared storage), *MyCluster* is the cluster to which your volume will belong, the name you're giving the file system will be *mysgfs2*, the number of journals will be set to two (the minimum possible is one), and the target block device will be */dev/vg0/mygfs2*.

If that you aren't going to have Pacemaker manage your GFS2 cluster, you'll need to mount it to a mount point. The cman cluster manager must already be running for this to work. The normal "mount" command will, similarly to OC2FS, actually invoke **mount.gfs2***.*

```
# mount /dev/vg0/mygfs2 /home/MyMountPoint
```

To ensure that your volumes are properly unmounted when a node shuts down - and assuming that you're not using Pacemaker to handle these things - you must have either loaded it through the **/etc/fstab** *file, or manually unmounted it with* **umount** *before the shutdown. Failure to perform either one of these actions could hang the system.*

And speaking of errors, being a journalled file system, recovery from a node failure is usually quick and painless. However, a single physical node that suddenly lost power or connectivity might require some bigger guns. **fsck.gfs2** will often be your weapon of choice. Now, since we're usually working with large data stores measuring in the terabytes, you'll need to be sure you've got enough available memory above and beyond what's already being used by the operating system. You'll also need to unmount your damaged volume before trying to repair it.

Usage of fsck is generally straightforward: and it will either work or it won't (although you should make sure that GFS2 file systems on all cluster nodes are unmounted).

```
# fsck.gfs2 -y /dev/vg0/mygfs2
```

There are plenty of other administrative tasks you can perform on a GFS2 system. **gfs2_grow**, for instance, will expand a mounted file system. gfs2_grow will lock a volume to prevent clients accessing its data during the operation.

```
# gfs2_grow /home/MyMountPoint
```

You apply gfs2_grow only after using LVM to expand the underlying logical volume. (Resizing an OCFS2 volume on the fly can be done through **tunefs.ocfs2**.)

You can add the number of journals kept on a file system using **gfs2_jadd**. This does not require that you first expand the underlying volume. The operation will fail, however, if the GFS2 file system itself is already full. This operation should be run on a file system that's mounted. You need to run it on only one node in the cluster, as its changes will automatically be propagated to the entire cluster.

You might first want to confirm how many journals are already contained:

```
# gfs2_tool journals /home/MyMountPoint
```

You can now **run jadd**, specifying the number of **new** journals you want to add.

```
# gfs2_jadd -j2 /home/MyMountPoint
```

gfs2_edit allows you to print or edit structural elements of an existing file system from the command line. Invoking **gfs2_edit** against a file system using only the -c argument will load an interactive editor. The editor has three working modes. Hex mode (which is the default) lets you work on file system blocks in hexadecimal and ascii. Structure mode lets you move through a representation of your file system to quick find individual values. Pointer mode will display additional information, like inode block pointers.

Hitting "m" will toggle between modes, "j" will jump between blocks, and "q" will escape the interface.

Command Cheat Sheet

Create DLM primitive	crm configure primitive dlm ocf:pacemaker:controld
Create Pacemaker group	crm configure group g_ocfs2mgmt controld o2cb
OCFS2 cluster layout conf	/etc/ocfs2/cluster.conf
OCFS2 policies	/etc/sysconfig/oc2cb
Start OCFS2 (direct)	service o2cb online
Start OCFS2 (Pacemaker)	crm resource start resource_name_ocfs2
Resize OCFS2 volume /dev/sda1	tunefs.ocfs2 -Q "UUID = %U\nNumSlots = %N\n"

Initialize partition	mkfs.ocfs2 -b 4K -C 32K -N 3 -L volumename /dev/sda4
Detect OCFS2 vol details	mounted.ocfs2 -d
Clone GFS2 config (via Pacemaker)	
	pcs -f MyDLM_cfg resource clone MyDLM clone-node-max=1
Show Pacemaker GFS resources	
	pcs -f MyDLM_cfg resource show
Activate GFS cluster (via Pacemaker)	
	pcs cluster cib-push MyDLM_cfg
Install GFS2 utilities	yum groupinstall "High Availability" "Resilient Storage"
Enlarge live GFS2 volume	gfs2_grow /home/MyMountPoint

Resources:

Project Home:	sourceware.org/cluster/gfs/
Documentation:	sourceware.org/cluster/doc/usage.txt

Other Storage Resources

OCFS and GFS2 are "shared-disk file systems" - in that they simultaneously access block level storage on all the nodes of a cluster. However, cluster storage can also work on distributed file systems that *replicate* data between nodes. These packages are of this latter type.

GlusterFS

GlusterFS (which, since 2014 has been rebranded as "Red Hat Gluster Storage") is free software based on multiple licenses that provides a network-attached storage file system. Servers are "storage bricks" running a glusterfsd daemon that mounts a local file system as glusterfs and replicates its data to other nodes. Clients connect over standard protocols like TCP/IP through the glusterfs client process that generates composite virtual volumes from multiple remote servers using stackable translators.

AFS (Andrew File System)

As a file-oriented distributed file system (rather than a block-oriented cluster), AFS - and it's open source OpenAFS branch - is scalable and location-independent and generates significantly less network traffic than NFS systems. It shares a location-transparent file name space among all clients on a cluster. Local files are written to the server only when closed by the client application. AFS relies on client cache and authenticates through Kerberos.

CephFS

Ceph is an open source distributed storage system that includes the RADOS (Reliable Autonomic Distributed Object Store) block storage service. RADOS works through autonomous, self-managing nodes replicating their data through a cluster. RBD - which interfaces with the host - is a distributed block device running within the Linux kernel on a KVM driver.

CephFS - now mostly developed in-house by Red Hat - is a free object storage solution that maintains data on a Ceph-based distributed cluster and presents client interfaces for storage on the object, block, and file, levels. Being distributed, it has no single point of failure, and is highly scalable. While its data stores are replicated and the system itself is self-healing, CephFS is not recommended for mission critical data because it lacks disaster recovery capabilities.

Test Yourself

1. OCFS2 nodes are defined in which file?

a) /etc/ocfs2/cluster.conf

b) /etc/default/cluster.conf

c) /etc/cluster.conf

d) /etc/ocfs2/default.conf

2. The value of "name" in which file must be identical to the contents of /etc/hostname?

a) default.conf

b) ocfs2.conf

c) cluster.conf

d) gfs2.xml

3. Which of these will properly apply an OCFS2 file system to the sda4 partition?

a) mkfs /dev/sda4

b) mk-ocfs2 /dev/sda4

c) mkfs-ocfs /dev/sda4

d) mkfs.ocfs2 /dev/sda4

4. What will the gfs2_grow /home/MyMountPoint command do?

a) Increase the size of a logical volume

b) Increase the number of inodes available to a file system

c) Increase the size of a mounted file system up to the maximum available space on its logical volume

d) Increase your IT department's HR budget

5. Which of the following commands will generate a configuration file for GFS2-Pacemaker integration?

a) pcs -f MyDLM_cfg resource create

b) pcs -f MyDLM_cfg resource show

c) pcs -f cluster cib MyDLM_cfg

d) pcs cluster cib MyDLM_cfg

Answer Key: 1:a,2:c,3:d,4:c,5:d

Alphabetical Index

CPSIA information can be obtained
at www.ICGtesting.com
Printed in the USA
LVOW02s0019200517

535221LV00003B/310/P